A USEFUL INHERITANCE

Studies in Epistemology and Cognitive Theory
Paul K. Moser, General Editor

Volume One

A Useful Inheritance

Evolutionary Aspects of the Theory of Knowledge

Nicholas Rescher

ROWMAN & LITTLEFIELD PUBLISHERS, INC.

ROWMAN & LITTLEFIELD PUBLISHERS, INC.

Published in the United States of America
by Rowman & Littlefield Publishers, Inc.
8705 Bollman Place, Savage, Maryland 20763

British Cataloging in Publication Information Available

Library of Congress Cataloging-in-Publication Data

Rescher, Nicholas.
A useful inheritance : evolutionary aspects of
the theory of knowledge / Nicholas Rescher.
p.   cm.
Includes bibliographical references.
1. Evolution.   2. Knowledge, Theory of.   I. Title.
BD177.R47   1990   121—dc20   89–27509 CIP

ISBN 0–8476–7615–3

5   4   3   2   1

Printed in the United States of America

 The paper used in this publication meets the minimum requirements of
American National Standard for Information Sciences—Permanence of
Paper for Printed Library Materials, ANSI Z39.48–1984.

For Tom Rockmore
Friend, Scholar, Gentleman

Contents

Preface

Evolutionary epistemology is a relatively recent phenomenon. To be sure, its antecedents go back to Darwin's *The Descent of Man* itself. But as an independent and well-defined project, it is a child of the post-war penchant for "interdisciplinary studies" characteristic of the second half of the twentieth century. No doubt, its biggest single impetus came from Karl von Frisch's pioneering investigation of information acquisition and transmission in bees, who utilize the polarization of scattered sunlight for orientation. Its acculturation to a philosophical context in the work of Konrad Lorenz serves to explain why evolutionary epistemology was initially more fashionable in Germany than elsewhere. Recently, however, its impact has spread rapidly around the globe.

In the hands of philosophers, evolutionary concerns tend to take on a somewhat different mein, since they are concerned not only with biological but also with cultural evolution. There should be no great difficulties about this, however. As war is too important to be left to the generals, so evolution is too important to be left to the biologists.

I began work on this project in the spring of 1987. But my interest in the field is much older, first manifesting itself in *Methodological Pragmatism* (Oxford, 1977). Various evolutionary themes and arguments have found their way into my subsequent books, and I thought that the time was now ripe to pull the various threads together to make up a more connected treatment of the topic. In particular, Chapter 2 is indebted to Chapter 9 of *Methodological Pragmatism* (Oxford,

1977), Chapter 4 to Chapter 5 of *The Riddle of Existence* (Lanham, 1984), and Chapter 5 to Chapter 11 of *The Limits of Science* (Berkeley and Los Angeles, 1984).

I am grateful to Christina Masucci, Linda Butera, Marian Kowatch, and Catherine Savel for their help in preparing a workable typescript for the publisher. And I am indebted to David Carey, Mark Notturno, and Michael Ruse for their generous aid in reading the book in draft form and suggesting various sensible improvements.

Nicholas Rescher
Pittsburgh, Penn.
February, 1989

ONE
Cognitive Evolution and Its Modes

SYNOPSIS

(1) *Homo Sapiens* is a rational animal, characterized as such by the fact that much of what people think and do proceeds under the formative guidance of intelligence. Our possession and use of intelligence can and should be understood on evolutionary principles, for intelligence constitutes our particular "competitive advantage" in the evolutionary scheme of things. (2) But while biological evolution accounts for our *possession* of intelligence, explaining the way in which we actually *use* it largely requires a rather different evolutionary approach, one that addresses the development of thought-*procedures* rather than that of thought-*mechanisms* as such. The two domains involve radically different modes of evolutionary process, the one "blind," and the other "teleological."

---

(1) Homo Sapiens: Intelligence as the Survival Mechanism of our Species

The ancients saw man as "the rational animal" (*zoōn logon echōn*), set apart from the world's other creatures by the capacity for speech and deliberation. Following the precedent of Greek philosophy, Western thinkers have generally deemed the deliberate use of knowledge for the guidance of our actions to be at once the glory and the duty of *homo sapiens*.

Humans have evolved within nature to fill the ecological niche of an intelligent being. This human intelligence of ours is the product of a prolonged process of biological evolution.

1

There are many ways for an animal species to make its way in the world. Diverse alternative modes of coping within nature present themselves to biological organisms: the routes of multiplicity, toughness, flexibility, and isolation, among others. But one promising evolutionary pathway is afforded by the route of *intelligence*, that of adapting by the use of the brain rather than brawn, by cleverness rather than power, by flexibility rather than specialization. A fertile ecological niche lies open to a creature that makes its way in the world not by sheer tenacity or by tooth and claw, but by intelligence—by coordinating its own doings and the world's way through cognitive foresight. Man's possession of intelligence and capacity for reason are readily understandable on evolutionary principles. For these resources are clearly a means to adaptive efficiency, enabling us—sometimes at least—to adjust our environment to our needs and wants, rather than the reverse. It is not all that difficult to visualize how intelligence—with its characteristic pursuit of cogency, efficiency, and optimality—can facilitate advantageous arrangements. Reason-deploying intelligence—the use of our brains to guide action by figuring out the apparent best alternative—is the survival instrument of our species in much the same way that other creatures ensure their survival by being prolific, or tough, or well-sheltered. Intelligence constitutes our particular "competitive advantage" in the evolutionary scheme of things. As Darwin himself stressed, in a competitive Darwinian world, a creature that can understand how things work in its environment and can exploit this understanding in action thereby secures an evolutionary edge.

Intelligence has evolved not because the emergence of intelligence is a purpose of nature, but because intelligence aids the survival of its possessors within nature (at any rate, up to a point, since a benign outcome to the nuclear arms race is not yet a foregone conclusion). Intelligence arises through evolutionary processes because it represents one effective means of survival. Intelligence is our functional substitute for the numerousness of termites, the ferocity of lions, or the toughness of microorganisms. The long and short of it is that we rational animals would not be here as the sorts of creatures we are and could not long continue in existence as such if our rationality were not survival-conducive.

Intelligence is not an inevitable feature of conscious organic life. Here on earth, at least, it is our peculiarly human instrumentality, a matter of our particular evolutionary heritage. Man is *homo quaerens*. With us, the imperative to understanding is something altogether basic; we cannot function, let alone thrive, without information regarding what goes on about us. The knowledge that orients our activities in this world is itself the most practical of things—a rational animal cannot feel at ease in situations of which it can make no cognitive sense. The demand for understanding, for cognitive accommodation to one's environment, for "knowing one's way about," is one of the most fundamental requirements of the human condition. The "discomfort of unknowing" is a natural human feeling and understandable as such. To be ignorant of what goes on about one is actually dangerous for the survival of a thinking creature. As William James wisely observed, "The utility of this emotional effect of expectation is perfectly obvious; 'natural selection,' in fact, was bound to bring it about sooner or later. It is of the utmost practical importance to an animal that he should have prevision of the qualities of the objects that surround him."[1]

Intelligence's penchant for the acquisition of information is one more facet of evolution's strategy of making what is useful to the species compelling to the individual by way of pleasure (want) or demand (need). We rational animals must feed our minds even as we must feed our bodies. In pursuing information, as in pursuing food, we have to make do with the best we can get at the time. We have questions and need answers: the best answers we can get here and now, regardless of their imperfections. It is this basic practical impetus to coherent information that underlies the two fundamental imperatives of cognitive intelligence:

(1) Do the best you can to obtain adequate answers to your questions,

(2) Feel free to accept those answers, to deem them worthy of credence, at least for the time being, proceeding on the principle that we must make do with the best we can get as good enough for present purposes.

Bafflement and ignorance—to give suspensions of judgment the somewhat harsher name that is their due—themselves exact a substantial price from us. The need for information, for cognitive orientation in our environment, is as pressing a human need as that for food itself, and more insatiable. We humans want and need our cognitive commitments to comprise an intelligible story, to give a comprehensive and coherent account of things. Cognitive vacuity, dissonance, or disorientation can be as distressing to us as physical pain.

Information represents a deeply practical requisite for us humans. A basic demand for understanding and cognitive orientation presses in upon us, and we are inexorably impelled towards (and are pragmatically justified in) satisfying that demand. The Norwegian Arctic explorer Fridjtof Nansen put it well. What drives men to explore the uninviting polar regions, he said, is

> the power of the unknown over the human spirit. As ideas have cleared with the ages, so has this power extended its might, and driven Man will-nilly onwards along the path of progress. It drives us in to Nature's hidden powers and secrets, down to the immeasurably little world of the microscopic, and out into the unprobed expanses of the Universe . . . it gives us no peace until we know this planet on which we live, from the greatest depth of the ocean to highest layers of the atmosphere.

This Power runs like a strand through the whole history of polar exploration. In spite of all declarations of possible profit in one way or another, it was that which, in our hearts, has always driven us back there again despite all setbacks and suffering.[2]

Thus, it is not particularly surprising that humans should succeed in acquiring information about the world. This is natural and to be expected, because if we did not succeed in this cognitive venture we wouldn't be here as the sort of creatures we are. The rationale for our cognitive resources is fundamentally Darwinian. Indeed, the conception of knowledge as a tool for survival—cognitive Darwinism—is as old as biological Darwinism. The master himself put forward the idea that man's capacities and competences in the area of language, reasoning, and theorizing are part and parcel of his biological endowment, emerging because these abilities were biologically advantageous in the struggle for survival.[3] And after Darwin this idea burst like a Roman candle across the firmament of nineteenth-century thought. The concept of evolution was applied to validate explanatory recourse to some intellectual resources by various of the major philosophers of the day, including Arthur Schopenhauer, Herbert Spencer, Charles Sanders Peirce, and a host of thinkers of otherwise variant persuasions who have also followed suit.[4]

(2) Varieties of Evolutionary Process

One important refinement of evolutionary epistemology is of later vintage, however; namely the development of an evolutionary approach with respect not only to our cognitive faculties as such but also to the very *content* of knowledge. For, since humans transmit to their offspring not only genetic traits, but also intellectual instrumentalities like concepts, beliefs, tools and methods, it is only natural that a process of selection should also operate at the aphysical, ideational level, and serves to favor survival of those cultural forms that prove to be the most serviceable.

An evolutionary process of development involves three primary factors that generate cross-generational replication over time: mechanisms for introducing variations ("mutations"); mechanisms for the elimination of certain such mutations ("selection"); and mechanisms for the preservation and/or propagation of the selected variations. And here there is an analogy between the biological and the sociological situations that is both close and far-reaching:

BIOLOGY	SOCIOLOGY
biological mutation	procedural variation
reproductive elimination of traits through their nonrealization in an individual's progeny	reproductive elimination of processes through their lapsed transmissions to one's successors (children, students, associates)
one's physical progeny	those whom one influences

On the one hand, we deal with the biological transmission of physical traits by biological inheritance across generations; on the other, with the social propagation of cultural traits by way of generation-transcending influence. But the fundamental structure of the process is the same on either side. Both involve the conservation of structures over time.

It must accordingly be recognized—and stressed—that the survival-conducive role in biological evolution of man's generic capacity for thought is not alone at issue with respect to cognitive matters. Evolution-like processes are also at work in the historical development of the concrete instruments and procedures of man's thinking. Not only our various capacities for intelligent operation, but even the way in which we go about using them, have an evolutionary basis—albeit in *ra-*

tional rather than *natural* selection. Even though biological evolution accounts of our *possession* of intelligence, accounting for much or most of the way in which we actually *use* it calls for a rather different evolutionary approach, one that addresses the development of thought-procedures rather than of the thinkers themselves. This sort of non-biological evolutionary epistemology also figures in our present deliberations, specifically as regards the cultural development of our instrumentalities of *conception.*

An evolutionary process must as such involve mechanisms of *mutation* and of *selection.* Mutation is needed to arrive at a plurality of (potentially competing) alternatives. Selection then enters in to provide for the survival of the somehow "fittest" alternative. Both these processes can in theory take one or another of two very different forms; the one blind, the other teleological (purposeful). Accordingly, there are two sorts of "mutations":

(1) "chance": *random* variation, blindly generated alternatives

(2) "contrivance": *purposeful* variation, a somehow "designed" variation in line with some governing goal, function, or objective

And there are also two sorts of selection processes:

(1) "natural": failure (absolute or statistical) to reproduce or replicate for *physical causes.*

(2) "rational": failure (absolute or statistical) to be perpetuated for *functional/rational reasons.*

Given this duality, four very different modes of evolution can in principle be contemplated:

	Mutation	Selection
Darwinian:	random	natural
Lamarckian:	random	rational
Bergsonian:	purposeful	natural
Teilhardian:	purposeful	rational

We shall not have occasion here to invoke the two "mixed" modes of Lamarckian and Bergsonian evolution. For the cases that will concern us are primarily those of *biological* evolution, which (so one may at this time of day suppose) takes the Darwinian form, and those of *cultural* evolution, which (as the discussion will try to substantiate) is rather different in character, and stands at the opposite end of the spectrum.

Biological evolution is undoubtedly Darwinian, with teleologically blind natural selection operating with respect to teleologically blind random mutations. Cultural evolution, on the other hand, is generally Teilhardian, governed by a rationally-guided selection among purposefully devised mutational variations.[6] Taken in all, cognitive evolution involves both components, superimposing rational selection on biological selection. Our cognitive capacities and faculties are part of the natural endowment we owe to biological evolution. But our cognitive methods, procedures, standards, and techniques are socio-culturally developed resources that evolve through *rational* selection in the process of cultural transmission through successive generations. Our cognitive hardware (mechanisms and capacities) develops through Darwinian natural selection, but our cognitive software (the methods and procedures by which we transact our cognitive business) develops in a Teilhardian process of rational selection that involves purposeful intelligence-guided variation and selection. Biology produces the instrument, so to speak, and culture writes the music—where obviously the former powerfully constrains the latter. (You cannot play the drums on a piano.)

Rational selection is a matter not of a *biological* but of a

rationally selective elimination (or *rationally* preferential retention) of a process of historical transmission that involves a
reasoned preference based on purposive consideration. A
rigorously biological eliminative model for methodological or
procedural evolution is unrealistic. For what is basically at
issue in this domain is the matter of historical survival based
on communal behavior in transmission through teaching and
example. As changes are entertained (under the pressure of
necessitating circumstance), one methodological instrument
may eventuate as more fit to survive than another, because
extensive experience shows that it answers better to the range
of relevant purposes. The ways in which we make use of our
biologically given capacities are cultural resources preserved
and transmitted by *social* preferences operative in example
and teaching. There is a preferential selection at work in the
perpetuation of those methods and procedures whose effectiveness is indicated by the lessons of experience. Whatever
may be the shortcomings of a rational selectionist approach
to biological evolution via genetic mechanisms, it is clearly
useful and appropriate for the cultural evolution operative in
the transmission of our intellectual resources.

Natural and rational selection are kindred processes. Even
as in biological evolution is a matter of the selective perpetuation through biological transmission over time within a
certain population of those physical traits that are favorable
to the continued existence of individuals, so in rational
evolution those methods (processes) are selectively perpetuated over time in teaching and borrowing from examples
favorable to the efficient achievement of tasks to whose
accomplishment the group is committed. And a deep kinship
obtains between the two evolutionary modes based on the
parallelism:

inherent mutation—procedural variation

inherent retention—rational retention

The processes of the left side combine to move the species towards superior "fitness," those on the right side combine to move procedural processes toward superior efficiency. On both sides alike, the evolutionary processes at issue exert a pressure in the direction of greater efficiency and effectiveness in niche-attunement: like the market in economics, evolution makes for an efficient and economic accommodation to the requirements of the prevailing circumstances.

In rational selection, however, the matter is one of *favoring* certain alternatives in the transmission process because these lead more readily to preferred results. This whole approach presupposes the picture of intelligent beings acting rationally with reference to ends-in-view. Where rational selection is operative, pragmatism and evolution walk hand-in-hand because those processes that are inherently advantageous (more efficient, effective, economical, etc.) will be more than likely the ones that survive to make their way down the corridor of time. The crux is the matter of what is deemed fitting to transmit because of its demonstrated efficacy in the harsh school of the lessons of experience.

Rational selection is accordingly a process of fundamentally the same *sort* as natural (biological) selection; both are devices for eliminating certain items from cross-generational transmission. But their actual workings differ, since elimination by rational selection is not telically blind and biological, but rather preferential/teleological and overtly rational. Orthodox Darwinian selection is, in effect, a way of *removing* teleology; it provides a way of accounting for *seeming* purposiveness in purpose-free terms, by deploying the mechanisms of a *blindly eliminative* annihilation of certain forms in place of any recourse to preferential considerations. But rational selection is something else again: it can operate only with respect to beings endowed with intelligence and action, with reasoning and purposes, its mechanism being the deliberate failure to perpetuate forms that are not purpose-serving.

Once intelligent creatures appeared on the scene, reproductive elimination as such no longer monopolizes the processes of development. Among rational creatures, cultural patterns that are inefficient decline from one generation to another because these processes are less effective at reproducing themselves, since people's attachment to these patterns becomes undermined because of this very fact of their inefficiency, ineffectiveness, avoidable cumbersomeness, or the like.

Our intelligence and our knowledge are the fruits of collective and cumulative effort. We humans cannot all and always begin at square one; life is too short. Most of what we have—physically and intellectually—is inherited from the past, and some part of what we ourselves do is in turn transmitted to the future. The social aspect of cultural evolution is paramount for our intellectual development. And it provides for a particularly potent instrumentality. Cultural evolution can manage to achieve things that biological evolution cannot—borrowing across geneological lines (that is, from "foreign" groups), for example—or effecting changes of operation within the boundaries of a single generation.

Evolutionary epistemology has two distinct, albeit interrelated, traditions. One, recently exhibited in K. R. Popper and more explicitly in Stephen Toulmin, is a matter of a cultural development involving an evolution-analogous approach according to which ideas battle for selection by the way of adoption and perpetuation in the human community through a process in which the fittest are likely to prevail. This, in effect, is cultural evolution by rational selection. The other, originated by Herbert Spencer and Charles Darwin and carried forward in C. S. Peirce, Karl von Frisch, and Konrad Lorenz, holds that the human mind has certain genetically determined innate dispositions to manage things in a particular way because this is conducive to survival. This represents paradigmatic biological evolution through natural selection.

Our overall deliberations will certainly have to take both

sorts of evolutionary process into view. But to begin with, we shall focus on some aspects of specifically *cultural* evolution. For while natural selection unquestionably accounts for man's possession of intelligence and reason, *rational* selection clearly accounts best for the characteristics of its use. Biological processes are ill-suited to accommodate the characteristic flexibility of intelligence as opposed to the programmed automatism of most modes of behavior encountered in the animal kingdom. Our methods of using intelligence develop selectively under the aegis of intelligence itself. However implausible a rationally teleological approach may be in strictly *biological* evolution, it is eminently and unproblematically tenable in *methodological* evolution in matters pertaining to the *modus operandi* of intelligent and rational beings. The historical emergence of our thought mechanisms is doubtless biological (Darwinian), but the development of our thought *methods* is governed by the social process of cultural evolution. And at this secondary, *procedural* stage biological and cultural evolution part ways to some extent. Thinking people are by and large just as interested in the future fate of their *ideas* as in the future fate of their descendents: the survival of their *values* is no less significant for them than that of their *genes*.

NOTES

1. William James, "The Sentiment of Rationality," in *The Will to Believe and Other Essays in Popular Philosophy* (New York: Longmans Green, 1897), p. 78.

2. Quoted in Roland Huntford, *The Last Place on Earth* (New York: Atheneum, 1985), p. 200.

3. "The small strength and speed of man, his want of natural weapons, etc., are more than counterbalanced, firstly, by his intellectual powers, through which he has formed himself weapons, tools, etc., though still remaining in a barbarous state, and, secondly, by his social qualities which lead him to give and receive aid

from his fellow men." *The Origin of The Species* (New York: Modern Library, 1952), pp. 443–44. Darwin elaborates on this greatly in *The Descent of Man* (New York: A. L. Bunt, 1874).

4. Among the many older writers who deserve recognition are J. M. Baldwin, Ludwig Boltzmann, H. S. Jennings, Ernst Mach, D. Lloyd Morgan, Georg Simmel, and Hans Vaihinger. For the more recent, very substantial literature of the field, see references provided in the bibliography to this book.

5. For a compact but useful conspectus of the former, here peripheral issue, see Abner Shimony, "Perception from an Evolutionary Point of View," *The Journal of Philosophy*, vol. 69 (1971), pp. 571–83.

6. Various aspects of cultural evolutions are interestingly treated in *Culture and the Evolutionary Process* by Robert Byrd and Peter J. Richardson (Chicago and London: University of Chicago Press, 1985). Their deliberations indicate that cultural evolution is not just an *analogue* of biological evolution, but that both are variant forms of one structurally uniform process.

TWO

Thesis Darwinism: A False Start in Evolutionary Epistemology

SYNOPSIS

(1) Karl Popper's theory of evolutionary epistemology is based on the idea that scientific discovery is the result of a trial-and-error elimination of blindly conjectured hypotheses. (2) This theory makes scientific progress an inexplicable, virtually miraculous phenomenon. (3) The fatal flaw of Popper's approach lies in the fact that its Darwinian evolutionism is addressed to *theses* (theories or hypotheses). Only an account that focuses on cognitive *methods*—and thereby automatically provides for rational rather than random selection—can offer an adequate basis for understanding the historical realities of scientific progress. (4) The methodological turn is needed to make evolutionary epistemology into a viable project, though its evolutionism is not a matter of *natural* selection among method-users but one of *rational* selection through a trial and error testing of our cognitive methods themselves.

(1) Popper's Model of Evolutionary Epistemology

One of the most elaborate and influential contemporary versions of evolutionary epistemology is the model of scientific progress presented in Popper's *Objective Knowledge* (Oxford, 1972). Popper geared his cognitive evolutionism specifically to *theories* and *hypotheses* considered with a view to their "fitness to survive by standing up to tests" (p. 19). His theory was based on a model of random conjecture and refutation,

15

its stance being as follows: Nature's doings can always be explained by various (in principle endlessly diverse) hypotheses. The scientist ventures a conjecture from this infinite range. But the subsequent testing of these hypotheses with a view to their falsification provides a process of "selection" among them. The basic idea of Popperian hypothesis-evolution calls for such a determination mechanism of blind cognitive variation and eliminative selection among scientific theories by "the method of trial and the elimination of errors" (p. 70).[1]

As Popper sees it, the dynamics of this evolutionary process involves cyclic movements: from initial problem to tentative theory to error-elimination to refined problem to refined tentative theory, and so on. "The neo-Darwinist theory of evolution is assumed: but, it is restated by pointing out that its 'mutations' may be interpreted as more or less accidental trial-and-error gambits, and 'natural selection' as one way of controlling them by error elimination" (p. 242). The trial-and-error search procedure at issue here is blind and essentially random.[2] According to Popper, the difference between Einstein and an amoeba is—from the epistemological standpoint—a matter of degree rather than kind, since "their methods of almost random or cloud-like trial and error movements are fundamentally not very different" (p. 247). Rather, the crucial difference between them lies in the sphere of reactions to solutions, because unlike the amoeba, Einstein "approached his own solutions *critically*" (p. 247) and subjected them to deliberate falsifying tests. As a result of this eliminative selection of hypotheses, "our knowledge consists, at every moment, of those hypotheses which have shown their (comparative) fitness by surviving so far in the struggle for existence; a competitive struggle which eliminates those hypotheses which are unfit" (p. 261).

As this summary indicates, Popper's model of scientific

inquiry via a process of random conjecture and eliminative refutation rests on a combination of three basic commitments:

(1) With respect to any given scientific issue endlessly many alternative hypotheses are in principle always available.

(2) Science proceeds by the trial-and-error elimination of haphazardly conjectural hypotheses.

(3) This selective elimination process is inductively blind: man has no inductive capability for discriminating good from bad hypotheses—of separating the promising from the unpromising, the inherently more plausible from the inherently less plausible. And there is never any reason to think that those hypotheses that have been proposed or considered are somehow more advantageous than those that have not. At every stage, our search among the alternatives is simply a matter of blind groping.

These three points present the salient features of Popper's theory of evolutionary epistemology. They at once define its nature and engender its problems.

(2) The Inexplicability of Scientific Progress on Popperian Grounds

Unfortunate consequences arise straightaway from Popper's approach. For if the situation is indeed as his various suppositions indicate, then we forthwith destroy any prospect of understanding the success of man's cognitive efforts. The whole immense achievement of natural science—its historically demonstrated ability to do its work well and to produce useful and impressively informative results—now becomes altogether unintelligible. Indeed, this success in furnishing explanatory theories that perform well in prediction and the guidance of applications in a complex world is now an accident of virtually miraculous proportions, every bit as fortuitous as someone's correctly guessing at random the telephone numbers of someone else's friends.

As Popper himself stresses, discovery of *truth* is the regulative ideal of the enterprise of inquiry (*Objective Knowledge*, pp. 29–30). But this creates grave difficulty. For how can Popperian error elimination ever possibly provide warrant for the conviction that our effort at inquiry involves a movement—however slow or hesitating—towards this ideal of truth? "We test for truth," so Popper maintains, "by eliminating falsehood." But clearly this would work only in the context of a theory of limited possibilities. (One can eliminate endless possibilities as solutions to a problem—say all those infinitely many odd integers as answers to a Diophantine problem whose real answer is eight—without thereby moving significantly closer to the truth.)

Once we grant that, as Popper time and again insists, any hypotheses we might actually entertain are but a few fish drawn from an infinite ocean of alternative possibilities—are only isolated instances of those infinitely many available hypotheses we have not even entertained, none if which are inherently less meritorious than those we have—then the whole idea of *seeking truth* by the elimination of error becomes pointless.[3] If infinitely many distinct roads issue from the present spot, then by ruling out one or two (or *n*) of these, we have come not one jot closer to finding the one that leads to the desired destination. The plain fact is that when theories and theses are at issue, then an evolutionary model of random variation and selective retention is in difficulty, because the range of alternative possibilities with which it must come to terms is simply too large for realistic manageability. Genuine blind variation among beliefs would generate a Laputan chaos from which no rational sense could be extracted.

However, Popper is deeply (and apparently proudly) committed to this unhappy aspect of his theory. For him, the success of science is something fortuitous, accidental, literally *miraculous*, and totally unintelligible:

> However, even on the assumption (which I share) that our quest for knowledge has been very successful so far, and that we now know something of our universe, this success becomes miraculously improbable, and therefore inexplicable; for an appeal to an endless series of improbable accidents is not an explanation. (The best we can do, I suppose, is to investigate the almost incredible evolutionary history of these accidents, from the making of the elements to the making of the organisms.) [*Objective Knowledge*, p. 204]

On the premises of Popper's theory of science, the question of an explanation of the success of science is met with a blank *ignorabimus* of intrinsic mystery. We are denied any prospect of a viable account of how the nature of the world and the nature of man's cognitive technology can conjoin to *explain* why our endeavors to acquire knowledge are as successful as they are.

All this, of course, holds only on the quixotically "democratic" view that all the possible hypotheses stand on an equal footing, that our process of selection is nowise shrewd but virtually random, that we are not to take the stance that those hypotheses we propose to treat seriously can reasonably be more promising candidates than the rest. In short, we must refrain from crediting the human intellect with any sort of inductively oriented *heuristic skill*, any capacity, however modest, for singling out those alternative hypotheses that are (likely to prove) more promising candidates than the rest. But if one is not entitled to regard hypothesis-elimination as narrowing the field of the *real* possibilities, then this entire eliminative process becomes probatively pointless. Popper's position is internally incoherent. The technique of error elimination is capable of serving the Popperian desideratum of leading closer to the truth only if one is willing to take the Popper-repugnant step of crediting inquiring intelligence with a capacity for doing reasonably well in the selection of hypothesis for testing—and thus as *not* constrained to operate by blind trial and error.

Popper explicitly and emphatically insists that "no theory of knowledge should attempt to explain why we are successful in our attempt to explain things" (*Objective Knowledge*, p. 23). And yet this self-denying ordinance is nowhere defended on the basis of an inexorable inevitability in the nature of things—the only sort of defense, surely, that could motivate the acceptance of so unpalatable and counterintuitive a doctrine. It is difficult to exaggerate the unsatisfactory nature of this position. It fails at the basic and rudimentary task of any adequate explanatory theory, that of "saving the phenomena" by providing some promising account for them.

But in forming such cultural artifacts as our cognitive modus operandi in belief-formation, the counsel of experience is clearly at work—past recesses and failures in handling issues analogous to those currently in hand. This aspect of cognitive evolution is clearly experience-guided rather than blind—in contrast to the development of cognitive *machinery* in biological evolution.[4]

Any adequate explanation of our ability to secure scientific knowledge of the world must combine a theory of nature and a theory of inquiry in such a way that it emerges as only natural and to be expected that an inquiry conducted along *those* lines should be successful. But the very best Popper can offer us here is the thought that our efforts to acquire information about the world by our investigative processes *may possibly* succeed: "That we cannot give a justification . . . for our guesses [i.e., scientific hypothesis and theories] does not mean we may not have guessed the truth; some of our hypotheses may well be true" (p. 30). Regarding the capacity of scientific inquiry to afford a true picture of reality, "it is not irrational to hope as long as we live—and actions and decisions are constantly forced on us" (p. 101). In the search for truth, the finding of something that "may well be true" deserves no celebration; it smacks of failure rather than success. And, clearly, *a not irrational hope* in the adequacy of science is not good enough: what is wanted is a *rationally based expectation*—not, to be sure, an airtight *guarantee*, but at least a *reasonable assurance* that the scientific route to the solution of our cognitive problems in the factual area offers the best available prospect.

The vitalistic opponents of a rigoristic Darwinism have traditionally objected that evolution has proceeded too quickly and unerringly in devising such highly survival-efficient instruments, e.g., the human eye, for the developmental process to have been wholly the result of natural selection working on random variation. As is illustrated by the "creative evolutionism" of Bergson, vitalists have always objected that the random-variation-cum-natural selection model of the evolutionary process does not provide an explanatory basis adequate to account for the rapidity of evolution. They have maintained that the operation of some sort of vital principle is needed to pull the evolutionary process in the right direction and at the right speed. Now in the case of *biological* evolution, this objection is doubtless untenable: all the evidence indicates the available timespan is large enough for the neo-Darwinian mechanisms of mutations and genetic selection to do their work. But genetic mutations are of limited variety—unlike the possibilities for hypothesis formation where literally endless variations are available. Biologically, it thus suffices to test out the full range of available alternatives; there is no need to explore the vast range of *possible* alternatives. But in the cognitive case the situation is altogether different in this regard. For here the timespan is just too short to account for the phenomenon of progress in terms of a random hit-or-miss search amidst infinite possibilities.[5]

The Popperian model of the growth of scientific knowledge through the falsification of hypotheses arrived at by blind trial-and-error groping is thus crucially deficient in being admittedly unable to account for the *reality*, let alone the *rate* of scientific progress. Yet, this very issue of the *rate and structure of scientific progress* is certainly among the basic phenomena that any adequate theory of scientific knowledge must be able to explain. A theory that insists on hiding this issue out of sight behind a veil of ignorance and intrinsic mystery blazons forth the clear marks of its own inadequacy.

It is not hard to discern the root source of the difficulties encountered by Popper's approach to scientific progress. For his evolutionary theory of knowledge postulates a mechanism of selection by trial and error that proceeds *at the level of individual scientific theses or theories.* And this microscopic concern with individual claims and contentions is its fatal weak spot. Popper holds that distinct factual theses are not somehow linked by inherent interrelationships of natural necessity—rigoristic empiricist that he is, he dismisses this sort of thing out of hand as obscurantist and illegitimate nonsense. Popper agrees with Hume that all factual theses are wholly independent except insofar as their mode of formulation may embody strictly logical interconnections (i.e., relationships of meaning). He stands committed to a fundamentally Humean view that—logical overlaps apart—factual theses stand atomistically disconnected from one another. And this confronts him with the insuperable problem of how the cohesive generality, orderliness, and systematicity of our scientific macro-knowledge could ever emerge from the scattered minutiae of thesis-testings within the very limited *span of time* that science has had at its disposal. There are *just too many* diverse imaginable hypotheses to be gone through in an inductively blind trial-and-error search. If indeed our only investigative resource were of this character, then it would have required nothing short of a pre-established harmony between scientific guesswork and the ways of nature to come as far as we have managed to do over so short a course of human history.[6]

Thus, Popper's theory faces a vitiating dilemma: he must choose between having the Darwinian selection process operate between all *conceivable* (i.e., theoretically available) theories or between all *proposed* (i.e., actually espoused) theories. With the former course there is the difficulty of accomplishing a virtually infinite task in a limited span of time. But with the second course there is the difficulty of relating the proposed to the proposable. The problem of accounting for substantial progress within a limited timespan can be solved only if one supposes some sort of human capacity for efficiency in hypothesis-conjecture—a kind of inductive skill—so that those hypotheses actually conjectured are, in fact, likely to prove among the intrinsically superior alternative. However prominent a role pure haphazard randomness may have played in the early days of the development of our physical apparatus for acquiring and processing information (our human senses and our brains), by the time it comes to the projection of explanatory beliefs and theories, the time for randomness is long past. Scientific knowledge is not and cannot be the process of guesswork that is random through and through.

But Popper is, of course, emphatically unwilling to concede any such inductive talent for superior hypothesis-conjecture, given his well-known antipathy to anything of inductive-confirmationist tendencies. And, consequently, he is driven onto the other horn of the dilemma: his blindly groping trial-and-error mechanism is saddled with having to grapple with the whole gamut of conceivable alternatives, and so becomes trapped in the problem of time-availability and unrationalizable rates of progress.[7]

(3) Comparison with Methodological Darwinism

Difficulties of this sort are left behind once the shift is made from a Darwinism of *theses* to a Darwinism of *methods*. For now we can suppose a trial-and-error model that operates not with respect to *possible* theses but with respect to *actual* methods of thesis-substantiation. On such a model, the course of evolution, however slow in the initial stages, is able to provide for very rapid eventual progress once *any* headway at all is made. Only a cognitive evolutionism, which—like the proposed methodological approach—is inherently oriented towards generalized instrumentalities, can successfully pull its way out of the quicksands in which a thesis-oriented evolutionary theory becomes mired.

The manifold of individual theses is just too large for a trial-and-error mechanism to work adequately. The random variation of statements and theses opens a Pandora's Box of infinitely numerous alternatives. But plausibility considerations can serve to avert a need for random groping. Only if we have good reason to believe that the process of elimination proceeds with respect to a delimited range of really optimal alternatives can this process of pursuing the vagaries of blind chance produce any truth-presumptive results. Consider an analogy:

> Girolano Cardano, a sixteenth-century mathematician with a Renaissance penchant for boasting, maintained that a monalphabetic substitution cipher of his own invention was unbreakable because of the large number of possible solutions that must be tested. (A monalphabetic substitution cipher is the simplest kind; each letter of the original message is replaced by one and only one cipher letter consistently throughout the whole message.) Since there are 26 letters, there are 26 factorial different ways of pairing plaintext letters with cipher letters, or approximately 11×10^{28} different possible solutions, a consideration that led Cardano to feel the safety of numbers.

Yet with a few hours' instruction in frequency analysis and anagramming, most amateurs can solve these ciphers in a matter of minutes. Such is the potency of method.[8]

A shrewd insight into principles of regulative regularity can cut down to reasonable proportions search-times that would require astronomical periods of time on a random trial-and-error basis.

Thus, it is important, even when we recognize the utility of the random trial-and-error technique in rational inquiry, that this be thought of not as a blind groping among *all conceivable* alternative theses and theories, but as a carefully guided search among the *really promising* alternatives.[9] Inquiry is not a process of setting a random generator to work to produce hypotheses for testing. Useful hypotheses emerge not from haphazard combinations but from the detection of patterns in the empirical data. They are not created *ex nihilo* by random groping: they are *constructed* upon a suitable methodological foundation. Once a cognitive method begins to acquire a fair record of success, it builds up credit in the bank of epistemic validation. Now its endorsements begin to be the beneficiary of a favorable presumption of innocent-until-proven-guilty rather than the reverse.[10] And so the method now provides not isolated items but systematic results. We avoid blind groping among endless possibilities by methods and techniques—systematic processes that make use of analogies, plausibilities, simplicities, and the like, that cut a complex imprint of cases down to manageable size. Without such methodological guidance we are driven to a "method" that is, in effect, tantamount to the absence of method, that "method of last resort" as it were, a merely random groping among the possibilities.[11]

The weaknesses of an evolutionary model of scientific inquiry based on thesis-oriented trial and error can thus be overcome by a cognitive Darwinism of the method-oriented sort mooted here, one that operates at a level of generality that is lacking when our attention focuses on particular theses. On such a methodological approach, the process of trial-and-error mutation and rational selection is not seen as operative primarily and in the first instance in regard to theories or theses themselves, but in regard to the procedural principles and rule-of-thumb heuristics used in their substantiation. The human imagination is fertile enough that at any given stage of inquiry the range of theoretically envisageable *hypotheses* is "more plentiful than blackberries." But experience teaches that where the solution of our cognitive problems is concerned, the range of available investigative and explanatory *methods* is emphatically limited, being radically circumscribed by the particular resources of the historical era which places only limited alternatives at one's disposal. General methods that have some discernible promise of success to recommend them are few and far between, and when the range of alternatives is manageably small, haphazard groping among the possibilities can be a sensible way to proceed. Blind variation and selective retention is indeed a promising procedure in cognitive development, but only when it proceeds at the wholesale level of process rather than the retail level of product.

Most of the characteristic difficulties of an evolutionary epistemology based on thesis Darwinism are consequently obviated when we make the shift to a method Darwinism. The prospects of a trial-and-error evolutionism are vastly improved at this methodological level of trying available alternative procedures for the realization of our ends, retaining those that prove effective in the course of experience. Beliefs do indeed enter into cognitive evolution, but only beliefs of a very special sort, namely, those about methods, whose enormous advantage lies in their many-sided applicability. Such *methods* can become "tried and true" through a variety of diversified applications in a way that outdistances the multi-sidedness of all but the most vague and indefinite *theses.*

In effect, the shift from *theses* to *methods*—and specifically, methods for thesis-substantiationism—enables us "to have it both ways." We avoid occultism by relying *at the methodological level* upon a strictly trial-and-error mechanism of learning through rational selection. The combination of a model of method-learning based on trial and error and of thesis-learning based on the use of methods makes it possible to have the best of both worlds.[12] It means that the venture of thesis-validation is not condemned to blind trial and error, but is guided by *heuristic principles of method,* involving the use of methods that have proven their effectiveness in the past, and whose application in present conditions thus embodies a fundamentally inductive commitment.

Sometimes, of course, our use of cognitive methods figures in situations of biological survival. Michael Ruse provides one cogent example:

> Consider two would-be human ancestors, one with elementary logical and mathematical skills, and the other without very much in that direction. One can think of countless situations, many of which must have happened in real life, where the former proto-human would have been a great selective advantage over the other. A tiger is seen entering a cave that you and your family usually use for sleeping. No one has seen the tiger emerge. Should you seek alternative accommodation for this night at least? . . . Analogously for mathematics. Two tigers were seen going into the cave. Only one came out. Is the cave safe? . . . [Again] one hominid arrives at the water-hole, finding tiger-like footprints at the edge, blood-stains on the ground, growls and snarls and shrieks in the nearby undergrowth, and no other animals in sight. She reasons: "Tigers! Beware!" And she flies. The second hominid arrives at the water, notices all of the signs, but concludes that since all of the evidence is circumstantial nothing can be proven.

"Tigers are just a theory, not a fact." He settles down for a good long drink. Which of these two hominids was your ancestor?[13]

But usually, what is at issue in the evolution of cognitive rules is not the survival of the rule-employers but rather that of the rules employed within an inquiring community that tends to adopt and transmit those rules of procedure that have proven to be functionally effective.

Given the preceeding critique of thesis Darwinism, someone may well object to the proposed method Darwinism as follows:

> Your argument against thesis Darwinism is (put roughly) that the *pace* of progress of science is too rapid to be plausibly accounted for by a process of trial-and-error selection among the available alternatives. But does this argument not hold against your own position? The success of science certainly indicates very substantial sophistication on the side of procedure and methodology, and is this not every bit as difficult to account for along the lines of a Darwinian trial-and-error as is progress on the side of accepted theses?

Clearly if this objection held good, this would be something serious, but—fortunately—it is badly flawed. The argument that "not enough time" is available for the realization of the observed progress through more or less random improvements tells very differently as between theses and methods. For thesis Darwinism requires a tremendous number of successive improvements, given the immense range of the claims at issue in the build-up of the sciences. It is this enormous number of successive iterations of the selection process that demands so much time with thesis Darwinism, and that makes the rapid progress of science appear virtually miraculous from this point of view. However, there is, by contrast, no reason why methodological improvement cannot proceed at a glacially sedate Darwinian pace. Then, when at last an even modestly effective method has finally been devised, any further development can clearly proceed with extreme rapidity as we make use of cognitive methods for their own improvement.

Think of an analogy: a slow and stumbling process may have lain behind the ultimately successful development of the technological method for human flight, but once the rudimentary beginnings of the venture were in hand, the further development of sophisticated aerial transport proceeded with astonishing speed, and in an almost routine way. Milennia separated Icarus from the Wright brothers, but the subsequent step to Werner von Braun took but a single generation. Free flight advanced from a range of a few dozen meters to astronomical distances with astounding rapidity. And there is no reason to believe that the case of cognitive rather than technically manipulative methods should not be similar. Once an even partially adequate method for the testing of factual theses has been contrived, there is every reason to think that human ingenuity will devise suitable occasions for putting it to use—to the great advantage of the rapid progress of knowledge. At the level of theses—of envisageable alternative explanatory hypotheses—one faces an embarrassment of riches that makes effective progress through randomized selection-processes unintelligible on any basis that does not call for suppositions rationally unpalatable to any mind of empiricist inclinations. But the situation is very different in the methodological case. Once an even modestly satisfactory inquiry method is at hand, progress at the thesis level can be very swift because of the inherent power and generality of such a method. Moreover, thanks to the cyclically self-corrective aspect of such a method, further substantial progress in the methodological side itself becomes a real prospect. For, of course, we can use our cognitive methods themselves to appraise their own performance and provide aid in further improvement.

(4) The Role of Trial and Error

The present critique of Popperian evolutionism was anticipated well before Popper's day not only in its general tendency but even in its details. It was envisioned by Charles Sanders Peirce, whose view of the matter deserves being quoted at considerable length:

> But how is it that all this truth has ever been lit up by a process in which there is no compulsiveness nor tendency toward compulsiveness? Is it by chance? Consider the multitude of theories that might have been suggested. A physicist comes across some new phenomenon in his laboratory. How does he know but the conjunctions of the planets have something to do with it or that it is not perhaps because the dowager empress of China has at that same time a year ago chanced to pronounce some word of mystical power or some invisible jinnee may be present. Think of what trillions of trillions of hypotheses might be made of which one only is true; and yet after two or three or at the very most a dozen guesses, the physicist hits pretty nearly on the correct hypothesis. By chance he would not have been likely to do so in the whole time that has elapsed since the earth was solidified. You may tell me that astrological and magical hypotheses were resorted to at first and that it is only by degrees that we have learned certain general laws of nature in consequence of which the physicist seeks for the explanation of his phenomenon within the four walls of his laboratory. But when you look at the matter more narrowly, the matter is not to be accounted for in any considerable measure in that way. Take a broad view of the matter. Man has not been engaged upon scientific problems for over twenty thousand years or so. But put it at ten times that if you like. But that is not a hundred thousandth part of the time that he might have been expected to have been searching for his first scientific theory.

You may produce this or that excellent psychological account of the matter. But let me tell you that all the psychology in the world will leave the logical problem just where it was. I might occupy hours in developing that point. I must pass it by. You may say that evolution accounts for the thing. I don't doubt it is evolution. But as for explaining evolution by chance, there has not been time enough.

However man may have acquired his faculty of divining the ways of Nature, it has certainly not been by a self-controlled and critical logic. Even now he cannot give any exact reason for his best guesses. It appears to me that the clearest statement we can make of the logical situation—the freest from all questionable admixture—is to say that man has a certain Insight, not strong enough to be oftener right than wrong, but strong enough not to be overwhelmingly more often wrong than right, into . . . nature. An Insight, I call it, because it is to be referred to the same general class of operations to which Perceptive Judgments belong. This Faculty is at the same time of the general nature of Instinct, resembling the instincts of the animals in its so far surpassing the general powers of our reason and for its directing us as if we were in possession of facts that are entirely beyond the reach of our senses. It resembles instinct too in its small liability to error, for though it goes wrong oftener than right, yet the relative frequency with which it is right is on the whole the most wonderful thing in our constitution.[14]

With magisterial shrewdness, Peirce puts his finger upon exactly the right point: an evolutionary model with respect to possible hypotheses just cannot operate adequately within the actual (or indeed any remotely realistic) timespan.[15] The only point at which our present position parts company with Peirce is in its explicit and deliberate substitution of the heuristic *methodology* of inquiry and substantiation in place of an otherwise mysterious capacity of *insight* or *instinct*.

In explaining the historical realities of cognitive progress one seems to be caught in a dilemma: *either* (1) one relies upon a model of the development of scientific theories by blind trial and error (in which case there just is no way of getting a plausible account of the historical realities of the rapidity of scientific progress); or (2) one is driven to the occult vitalism-reminiscent *deus ex machina* device of an uncanny and inexplicable talent on the part of the inquirers for hitting near the truth of things.[16] But the presently envisioned methodological approach slips between the horns of this dilemma. In taking the methodological turn we are able to have it both ways. We can accept a model of cognitive progress based on the mechanism of pure trial and error. But by reorienting its applicability from *theses* (theories) towards *methods* for their substantiation, we are able to account for the rapidity of scientific progress in straightforward methodological terms. Accordingly, the orientation towards methodology makes it possible to resolve the problems encountered on the orthodox thesis-oriented approaches to evolutionary epistemology.

At the retail level, *individual* beliefs can certainly be biologically survival-conducive for truth-irrelevant reasons—as, for example, with ethical or religious beliefs that promote mutual support and solidarity in social groups. Both at the wholesale level of belief-forming methods that are employed systematically in a myriad of cases, there is bound to be linkage between adequacy and cultural survival in a community of rational inquirers.

To be sure, Darwinian processes have left us in possession of various thought-tendencies that are erroneous and misleading as to the actual facts. Not only are there sensory illusions (such as the whole range of optical illusions), but there are thought-illusions as well. Some of these relate to probability reasoning, as for example the "gambler's fallacy" of thinking that in repeated trials an outcome that has not occurred in a long time is therefore the more likely to arise in the near future. Another is the "pattern unlikelihood illusion" that sees the boy-girl birth order GGGBBBGGGBBB as less likely in a succession of hospital births than the more irregular-looking GGBGBGGBBGBG.[17]

But, of course, once our *methods* for the substantiation of the myriad of actuality-oriented (rather than probability-oriented) beliefs are well in place, then we are also in a position to amend and improve such misleading tendencies of thought.

Moreover, the supposition that methodological progress might proceed purely and solely by blind trial and error (i.e., by wholly random and rationally unguided variation) unquestionably goes too far. After all, methodological innovation is never wholly haphazard. In *any* area of endeavor—be it woodworking or chess or the cognitive project of fact-substantiation—methodological considerations pivot on the matter of functional efficacy. It makes sense to conceive of the issue of methods on analogy with the enterprise of engineering machine-tools, i.e., machines for making machines. For here too the quest for effectiveness comes into operation. This meta-methodological aspect of the matter serves to provide a workable account for the rapid pace of cognitive progress in terms of an evolutionary model oriented towards methods rather than theses—a model in which rational variation as well as rational selection plays a decisive part.[18]

NOTES

1. This resort to the mechanism of trial and error as a basic model for the theory of scientific method is not confined to Popperians. Stephen C. Pepper, for example, also maintained that "the inductive methods of experimental science are essentially systematized trial and error," and he based on this idea a rather sophisticated Darwinian model of intellectual processes. See his book, *The Sources of Value* (Berkeley and Los Angeles: Univ. of California Press, 1958), whence the preceding quote—from p. 106.

2. In Popper's book there is a stress on mutation-reminiscent randomness or near-randomness ("more or less accidental trial-and-error gambits," "almost random or cloud-like trial-and-error movements") that is revoked in Popper's Schilpp essay (*The Philosophy of Karl Popper*, ed. by P. A. Schilpp, 2 vols., La Salle: Open Court 1974). "I regard this idea of the 'blindness' of the trials in a trial-and-error movement as an important step beyond the mistaken idea of random trials" (p. 1062). But while Popper's *motive* for the change is clear enough, its dire implications for the whole tenor and tendency of his position are simply ignored.

3. Here there is a substantial disanalogy with the evolutionary case. Darwin did not need to include unicorns in the purview of the theory and explain their non-existence by some process akin to an account for the extinction of dinosaurs.

4. Many of the considerations involved by the opponents of evolutionary epistemology—the speed and growth of knowledge, the fact that the testing of theories is an intentional activity geared to such cognitive aims as explanation and prediction—can in fact be converted into arguments for the appropriateness in this domain of a cultural rather than biological model of evolution. See, for example, Paul Thagard, "Against Evolutionary Epistemology," *Proceedings of the Philosophy of Science Association: PSA, 1980*, ed. by P. D. Asquith and R. N. Giere (East Lansing: Philosophy of Science Society, 1980), pp. 187–96.

5. Popper is by no means wholly unaware that this problem of the rate of scientific progress involves difficulties for his theory. His discussion (on pp. 281–84) of the large-scale evolutionary leaps represented by the theory of "hopeful monsters" of R. B. Goldschmidt (*The Material Basis of Evolution* [New Haven: Yale University Press, 1940]) seems to recognize that a piecemeal progress advancing, so to speak, thesis by thesis may not be able to account for the speedy efficiency of scientific advance, and his discussion of the issue acknowledges that "this Darwinean theory of hopeful behavioral monsters 'simulates' not only Lamarckism but Bergsonian vitalism also" (p. 284; cf. also p. 270). But it emerges from the whole tenor of his deliberations that the machinery of "hopeful monsters" is itself just that—a hopeful monster, a *deus ex machina* introduced to save the theory from inherent difficulties which the

resources of its fundamental commitments have been unable to avert. On yet another occasion Popper seems to withdraw (in a footnote) from the reliance on the methodology of purely random trial and error that predominates throughout the body of his theory as developed in the main text. This footnote reads as follows:

> The method of trial and error-elimination *does not operate with completely chance-like or random trials* (as has been sometimes suggested), even though the trials may look pretty random; there must be at least an "after-effect" (in the sense of my *The Logic of Scientific Discovery*, pp. 162 ff.). For the organism is constantly learning from its mistakes, that is, it establishes *controls* which suppress or eliminate, or at least reduce the frequency of, certain *possible* trials (which were perhaps *actual* ones in its evolutionary past) (*Objective Knowledge, op. cit.*, p. 245, note 55.)

It is easy enough to see why Popper wants to take this line, but a difficult dilemma remains with regard to his ability to do so: (1) If the only ones among possible trials that can be bypassed are *actual past tests* and perhaps their very close cognates (in the manner of an "after-effect"), this cannot cut deeply enough into this immense multitude of available alternatives to do much good; (2) but if one concedes the existence of a (rationally cogent and unwarranted) learning process that can make really massively effective reductions in the range of alternatives that need consideration, then this resort of an "inductive talent" runs counter to the whole tenor of Popper's anti-inductivist program, which renders us impotent to carry the case-inductive strategy over from one situation to another. If *this* sort of device is needed to make the program work, then it effectively self-destructs.

6. This "too little time" complaint is reminiscent of the objections that William Thomson, Lord Kelvin at one time offered against Darwinian evolution on the grounds that—as he put it in his Presidential Address to the British Association in 1871—its mechanism of natural selection is "too like the Laputan method for making books, and that it did not sufficiently take into account a continually guiding and controlling intelligence." However inappropriate this objection might be deemed in the case of *biological* evolution, the situation would be quite otherwise in the case of

cognitive evolution. For an interesting account of the time-availability dispute between physicists on the one side and biologists and geologists on the other see Stephen G. Brush, "Thermodynamics and History" in *The Graduate Journal*, (1969), vol. 2, pp. 447–565.

7. In various sorts of situations, a search process based on blind guesswork can lead to highly sophisticated and "adaptive" solutions in the end. (See, for example, Richard Dawkins' *The Blind Watchmaker* [New York: Norton, 1986], esp. Chap. 3.) But this is because in such contexts we are able—as in the game of "20 Questions"—to make governing assumptions about the structure of the domain at issue. And this is something we are unable to do with respect to induction at large on a Popperian, anti-inductivist basis, though not (for example) on a Peircean approach, where we suppose *ab initio* an inductive talent that coordinates judgmental tendencies with objective likelihoods. In this case, we suppose that "pure guesswork" is not a matter of altogether blind and random groping among theses, but represents a process which we have reason, on independent grounds, to consider to be relatively efficient. And then we deal with a justificatory strategy that is *methodological* rather than *logical*.

8. See David Kahn, *The Codebreakers* (New York: Macmillan 1967), p. 143.

9. This represents a crucial disanaology between biological and cognitive evolution indicative of the quasi-"vitalistic" character of the latter. In biological evolution the mutations that actually arise fall across the entire spectrum of possible alternatives with equal probability, and so the direction of evolution is not determined by the direction of mutation: "It is emphatically selection, not mutation, that determines the direction of evolution," and if this were not so, then "it would be necessary to suppose that such mutations must be predominantly favourable" (Gavin de Beer, "The Darwin-Wallace Centenary," *Endeavor*, vol. 17 [1958], pp. 61–76; see p. 68). In the case of cognitive evolution *viewed from the standpoint of thesis-acceptance*, the case is exactly opposite: the actualization of possible mutant alternatives is probabilistically skewed, favorable mutations predominate, and the direction of evolution is governed as much by the inherent selectivity of mutation as by selection proper. But, as we shall see, in the cognitive case—unlike the biological—there is nothing occult about any of this, because one

can in principle imbed the "vitalistic" features of epistemological evolution at the thesis level within an orthodoxly randomized and blindly unguided evolutionary model at the methodological level.

10. See Chapter XII of the author's *Methodological Pragmatism* (Oxford: Blackwell, 1977).

11. The issues of this problem-area have perhaps been pursued more effectively by Herbert A. Simon than by any other current cognitive theoretician. See his essay "Does Scientific Discovery Have a Logic?" (*Philosophy of Science*, vol. 40 [1973], pp. 471–80), where further references to his work are given. One key summary runs thus: "The more difficult and novel the problem, the greater is likely to be the amount of trial and error required to find a solution. At the same time, the trial and error is not completely random or blind; it is, in fact, highly selective" (*The Sciences of the Artificial* [Cambridge, Mass.: MIT Press, 1969], p. 95). Exploration of the computer simulation of the processes of human learning and discovery brings clearly to light the operation of a heuristic of an essentially regulative/methodological kind. It is based on principles (such as the priority of "similarity" augmenting transformations in problem-solving) which *qua* theses are clearly false (are heuristic "fictions" in the sense of Hans Vaihinger), but which prove methodologically effective.

12. The methodological approach can thus lay claims to resolving the issue perceptively posed by Donald T. Campbell in the following terms: "Popper has, in fact, disparaged the common belief in "chance" discoveries in science as partaking of the inductivist belief in directly learning from experience. . . . [T]hat issue, and the more general problem of spelling out in detail the way in which a natural selection of scientific *theories* is compatible with a dogmatic blind-variation-and-selective-retention epistemology remain high priority tasks for the future." (P. A. Schillpp, ed., *The Philosophy of Karl Popper* [2 vols.; La Salle, 1974], p. 436). The present theory provides a natural basis for combining a natural selection process at the level of *theories* with an epistemology of blind-variation-and-selective-retention at the level of *methods*.

13. Michael J. Ruse, *Taking Darwin Seriously* (Oxford: Blackwell 1986), p. 162.

14. *Collected Papers*, vol. V, secs. 5.172–3. Compare the follow-

ing passage: "Nature is a far vaster and less clearly arranged repertory of facts than a census report; and if men had not come to it with special aptitudes for guessing right, it may well be doubted whether in the ten or twenty thousand years that they may have existed their greatest mind would have attained the amount of knowledge which is actually possessed by the lowest idiot." (*Ibid.*, vol. II, sec. 2.753.)

15. This point deserves emphasis. Most writers on induction who hold that man has (or develops) inductive skills do so in order to secure a nontrivial a priori probability for our conjectures for the purpose of Bayesian argumentation. Peirce, however, sees that this is also needed to rationalize the relatively rapid rate of scientific progress. On this aspect of Peirce's thought compare Robert Sharpe, "Induction, Abduction, and the Evolution of Science," *Transactions of the Charles S. Peirce Society*, vol. 6 (1970), pp. 17–31.

16. As one knowledgeable theoretician has said, "All existing learning theories contain explicit or implicit assumptions about some selective principle operating on initially random responses" (Donald T. Campbell, "Adaptive Behavior From Random Response," *Behavorial Science*, vol. 1 [1956], pp. 105–10).

17. Various other such delusions are detailed in the work of Daniel Kahnemann and Amos Tversky. See, for example, their paper, "Judgments of and by Representativeness," in Daniel Kahnemann, Paul Slovic, and Amos Tversky, eds., *Judgment under Uncertainty: Heuristics and Biases* (Cambridge, Mass.: MIT Press, 1982), p. 87, and also their "Belief in the Law of Small Numbers," *ibid.*, p. 24, as well as their "Judgement under Uncertainty, Heuristics and Biases," *Science*, vol. 125 (1974), pp. 124–31. Also see L. D. Phillips and W. Edwards, "Conservatism in Simple Probability Inference Tasks," *Journal of Experimental Psychology*, vol. 72 (1966), pp. 346–57.

18. Some of the ideas of this chapter are developed more fully in the author's *Methodological Pragmatism* (Oxford: Blackwell, 1977).

THREE

The Cultural Evolution of Communal Practices in Inquiry

SYNOPSIS

(1) Unlike biological evolution, cultural is teleological in nature. Our cognitive methods and procedures (software)—in contrast to our cognitive faculties and capacities (hardware)—emerge through a process of *rational* rather than Darwinian *natural* selection. (2) In particular, the emergence of trust and collaboration in inquiry is provided for by considerations of cost-effectiveness relative to the aims of the enterprise. Any communicatively interacting group of intelligent inquirers is bound to develop into a collaborating community under the pressure of self-interest. (3) The practices that characterize the operations of a scientific community should be seen as the products of such a purposively canalized cultural evolution based on rational selection.

(1) Cultural Evolution as a Teleological Process: Rational Selection

Scientifically-minded epistemologists nowadays incline to consider how the workings of the "mind" can be explained in terms of the operations of the "brain."[1] But this approach has its limits. Biological evolution is doubtless what accounts for the cognitive machinery whose functioning provides for our *possession* of intelligence, but explaining the ways in which we *use* it largely calls for a rather different sort of evolutionary approach, one that addresses the development of thought-procedures rather than that of thought-mechanisms—of "software" rather than "hardware." What is at issue here is a matter of cultural-teleological evolution through a process of *rational* rather than Darwinian *natural* selection. Very different processes are accordingly at work, the one as it were blind, the other purposive. (In particular, biological evolution reacts only to *actually realized* changes in environing conditions: cultural evolution in its advanced stages can react also to *merely potential* changes in condition through people's capacity to think hypothetically and thereby to envision "what could happen if" certain changes occurred.) Once intelligence appears on the scene to any extent, no matter how small, it sets up pressures towards the enlargement of its own scope, powerfully conditioning any and all future cultural evolution through the rational selection of processes and procedures on the basis of purposive efficacy.

Rationality—the intelligent management of matters of self-interest—thus emerges as the key factor in the evolutionary development of *methods* as distinguished from *faculties*. The "selective" survival of effective methods is no blind and mechanical process produced by some inexorable agency of nature; rational agents place their bets in theory *and* practice in line with methods that prove themselves successful, tending to follow the guidance of those that succeed and to abandon— or readjust—those that fail. Once we posit a method-using community that functions under the guidance of intelligence—itself a factor of biologically evolutionary advantage— only a short step separates the pragmatic issue of the applicative success of its methods (of *any* sort) from the evolutionary issue of their historical survival. As long as these intelligent rational agents have a prudent concern for their own interests, the survival of relatively successful methods as against relatively unsuccessful ones is a foregone conclusion.

The rational selection of methods and procedures is a complex process that transpires not in a "population" but in a *culture*. It pivots on the tendency of a community of rational agents to adopt and perpetuate, through example and teaching, practices and modes of operation that are relatively more effective than their available alternatives for the attainment of given ends. Accordingly, the historical development of methods and modes of operation within a society of rational agents is likely to reflect a course of actual improvement. Rational agents involved in a course of trial and error experimentation with different processes and procedures are unlikely to prefer for adoption by themselves and for transmission to their successors practices and procedures that are ineffective or inefficient.

This line of consideration does not envision a direct causal linkage between the historical survival of method users and the functional effectiveness of their methods. The relationship is one of common causation. The intelligence that proves itself survival-conducive also favors functional efficacy. In consequence, survival in actual use of a method within a community of (realistic, normal) *rational* agents through this very fact affords evidence for its being successful in realizing its correlative purposes.[2]

These deliberations regarding rational selection have to this point been altogether general in their abstract bearing upon methodologies of any shape or description. They apply to methods across the board, and hold for methods for peeling apples as much as for methods for substantiating knowledge-claims. But let us now focus more restrictedly on specifically *cognitive* methods, and consider the development of the cognitive and material technology of intellectual production.

There is every reason to think that the cognitive methods and information-engendering procedures that we deploy in forming our view of reality evolve selectively by an historic, evolutionary process of trial and error—analogous in role to though different in character from the biological mutations affecting the bodily mechanisms by which we comport ourselves in the physical world. An inquiry procedure is an *instrument* for organizing our experience into a systematized view of reality. And as with any tool or method or instrument, the paramount question takes the instrumentalistic form: does it work? does it produce the desired result? is it successful in practice in relation to the acquisition and development of information? This sort of legitimation lies at the basis of the cultural development of our cognitive resources via the variation and selective retention of our epistemically oriented intellectual products.[3]

It is clear that there are various alternative approaches to the problem of determining "how things work in the world." The examples of such occult cognitive frameworks as those of numerology (with its benign ratios), astrology (with its astral influences), and black magic (with its mystic forces) indicate that alternative explanatory frameworks exist, and that these can have very diverse degrees of merit. Now in the Western tradition the governing standards of human rationality are implicit in the goals of *explanation*, *prediction*, and, preeminently, *control*. (Thus the crucial factor is not, for example, sentimental "at-oneness with nature"—think of the magician vs. the mystic vs. the sage as cultural ideals.) These standards revolve about considerations of *practice* and are implicit in the use of our conceptual resources in the management of our affairs.

Given the reasonable agent's well-advised predilection for *success* in one's ventures, the fact that the cognitive methods we employ have a good record of demonstrated effectiveness in regard to explanation, prediction, and control is not surprising but only to be expected: the community of rational inquirers would have given them up long ago were they not comparatively successful. The effectiveness of our cognitive methodology is thus readily accounted for on an evolutionary perspective based on rational selection and the requirements for perpetuation through adoption and transmission.

Yet, people are surely not all that rational—they have their moments of aberration and self-indulgence. Might not such tendencies selectively favor the survival of the ineffective over the effective—of the fallacious rather than the true—and slant the process of cognitive evolution in inappropriate directions? C. S. Peirce certainly recognized this prospect:

> Logicality in regard to practical matters . . . is the most useful quality an animal can possess, and might, therefore, result from the action of natural selection; but outside of these it is probably of more advantage to the animal to have his mind filled with pleasing and encouraging visions, independently of their truth; and thus, upon unpractical subjects, natural selection might occasion a fallacious tendency of thought.[4]

However, the methodological orientation of our approach provides a safeguard against an unwarranted penchant for such fallacious tendencies. At the level of individual beliefs "pleasing and encouraging visions" might indeed receive a survival-favoring impetus. But this unhappy prospect is effectively removed where a *systematic* method of inquiry is concerned—a method that must by its very synoptic nature lie in the sphere of the pragmatically effective.

It is not difficult to give examples of the operation of evolutionary processes in the cognitive domain. The intellectual landscape of human history is littered with the skeletal remains of the extinct dinosaurs of this sphere. Examples of such defunct methods for the acquisition and explanatory utilization of information include astrology, numerology, oracles, dream-interpretation, the reading of tealeaves or the entrails of birds, animism, the teleological physics of the pre-Socratics, and so on. No doubt, such practices continue in operation in some human communities to this very day, but clearly not among those dedicated to serious inquiry into nature's ways—i.e., scientists. There is nothing intrinsically absurd or inherently contemptible about such unorthodox cognitive programs—even the most occult of them have a long and not wholly unsuccessful history. (Think, for example, of the prominent role of numerological explanation from Pythagoreanism, through Platonism, to the medieval Arabs, down to Kepler in the Renaissance.) Distinctly different scientific methodologies and programs have been mooted: Ptolemaic "saving the phenomena" vs. the hypothetico-deductive method, or again, Baconian collectionism vs. the post-Newtonian theory of experimental science, etc. The emergence, development, and ultimate triumph of that scientific method of inquiry and explanation invite an evolutionary account, though clearly one that involves rational rather than natural selection.

The objection looms: "But how can you say that evolutionary survival among cognitive methods is inherently rational? Hasn't astrology survived to the present day—as its continuing presence in newspaper columns attests?" The response runs: Astrology has indeed survived, but *not* in the scientific community, that is, not among people dedicated in a serious way to the understanding, explanation, and control of nature. In the Western, Faustian[5] intellectual tradition of science, the ultimate arbiter of rationality is represented by the factor of knowledge-wed-to-action, and the ultimate validation of our beliefs lies in the combination of theoretical and practical success—with "practice" construed primarily in its pragmatic sense. All these "occult" procedures may have survived in some ecological niche in Western culture, but in *science* they are long extinct and we no longer use them for the guidance of significant action.

We shall have occasion to note (in ch. four) that nature is an error-tolerant environment, so that people who form their ideas in imperfect ways will—up to a point—be able "to get away with it." But the pivotal point is that our invocation of rational selection has been geared specifically to the aims and purposes involved in scientific inquiry: prediction, systematic explanation, and control over nature. In other enterprises that have other purposes in view, rational retention may well point in other directions. (Who wants poetry written "on scientific principles?") But that nowise conflicts with the cogency of the present account in its own appropriate context.

Admittedly, the scientific approach to factual inquiry is simply one alternative among others, and it does not have an unshakable basis in the very constitution of the human intellect. Rather, the basis of our historically developed and entrenched cognitive tools lies in their (presumably) having established themselves in open competition with their rivals. It has come to be shown before the tribunal of bitter experience—through the historical vagaries of an evolutionary process of selection—that the accepted methods work out most effectively in actual practical *vis-à-vis* other tried alternatives.

An individual's heritage comes from two main sources: a biological heritage derived from the parents and a cultural heritage derived from the society. However, in the development of our knowledge, this second factor becomes critical. To establish and perpetuate itself in any community of *rational* agents, a practice or method of procedure must prove itself in the course of experience. Not only must it be to some extent effective in realizing the pertinent aims and ends, but it must prove itself to be more efficient than comparably available alternatives. With societies composed of rational agents, the pressure of means-end efficacy is ever at work in forging a process of cultural (rather than natural) selection for replacing less by more cost-effective ways of achieving the group's committed ends—its cognitive ends emphatically included. Our cognitive faculties are doubtless the product of biological evolution, but the processes and procedures by which we put them to work are the results of a *cultural* evolution that proceeds through rationally guided trial and error in circumstances of a pragmatic preference for retaining those processes and procedures that prove theorists efficient and effective.[6] Rational people have a strong bias for what works. And progress is swift because once rationality gains an inch, it takes a mile. Of course, cultural evolution is shaped and canalized by constraints that themselves are the products of biological evolution. For our instincts, inclinations, and natural dispositions are all programmed into us by evolution. The transition from a biologically advantageous economy of effective physical effort to a cognitively advantageous economy of effective intellectual efforts is a short and easy step.

(2) The Rationale of Trust and the Emergence of Collaboration

The historical development of the social processes and practices that characterize the conduct of inquiry in its institutionalized setting in the domain of science affords a clear illustration of this phenomenon of rational selection. In any community of interacting rational agents, the pragmatic impetus conduces powerfully to the selection and retention of those practices that prove themselves to be teleologically successful and functionally cost-effective in realizing the shared aims of the enterprise at hand. The *modus operandi* of the scientific community affords a clear illustration of this state of affairs.

Consider, for example, such customary practices of scientists as information sharing and open publication, a credit system based on the principle that being first is everything, and a rigoristic intolerance of plagiarism, cheating,[7] data forgery, and other modes of dishonesty. Rational selection militates towards their emergence and consolidation among scientists because all such practices are cost-effective relative to the goal structure of the scientific enterprise.

In particular, the development of the institutional ground-rules of science can best be understood on this basis. Once the impetus to systematic inquiry emerges in a human community (as the nature of the human condition renders it only natural that it should eventually do someplace or other), the efficient pursuit of the aims and objectives of the enterprise will engender the emergence—in a community of rational agents—of the sorts of practices of cooperation that characterize the operational code of the natural sciences. Science is indeed a project of cooperation and collaboration. But its motive force is self-interest, since by being helpful to others we are, to all intents and purposes, helping them to be helpful to us.

Contrast two hypothetical communities: The Trusters and the Distrusters. The Trusters operate on the principle: "Be candid yourself. And accept what other people say as truthful—at any rate in the absence of counterindications." The Distrusters operate on the principle: "Be deceitful yourself. And look on the assertions of others in the same light—as ventures in deception and deceit. (Even when ostensibly being truthful, they are only trying to lure you into a false sense of security.)" It is clear at once that the policy of the Distrusters is totally destructive of communication. If the accession of information for the enhancement of our knowledge through communication and exchange is the aim of the enterprise, the process of distrust is totally counterproductive. In intellectual as in financial commerce, trust is essential to the maintenance of universally beneficial institutions.

Not only is the maintenance of credibility an asset to communication, but some degree of it is in fact an outright necessity. The precept: "Protect your credibility; do not play fast and loose with the social groundrules, but safeguard your place in the community of communicators" is basic to the entire project of communication. And so, practices that discernibly lead in this direction are for that very reason the more likely to be tried and, once tried, retained.

A society of communicators is accordingly destined to

evolve under the pressure of rational self-interest into a kind of mutual-aid association whose members are engaged in a collaboration to create and maintain a fabric of trust. For, clearly, everyone benefits from a system (*modus operandi*) that maintains the best balance of costs and benefits for each of us in this matter of creating a communally usable pool of information.

It is easily seen that a contrary practice—one that takes a sceptical or agnostic stance towards the declarations of others—would be disastrous. For if, instead of treating those with whom one communicates on the basis of "innocent until proven guilty," one were to treat them on the lines of "not trustworthy until proven otherwise," this procedure would clearly prove vastly less economic. We would now have to go to great lengths in independent verification before we could achieve any informative benefits from the communicative contributions of others.

We know that various highly "convenient" principles of knowledge-production are simply false:

—What seems to be, is.

—What people say is true.

—The simplest patterns that fit the data are actually correct.

We realize full well that such generalizations do not hold—however nice it would be if they did. Nevertheless, throughout the conduct of inquiry we accept them as principles of *presumption*. We follow the higher-level meta-rule: "In the absence of concrete indications to the contrary, proceed as though such principles were true—that is, accept what seems to be (what people say, etc.) as true." The justification of this step as a measure of practical procedure is not the factual consideration that, "In proceeding in this way, you will come at correct information—you will not fall into error." Rather it is the methodological justification: "In proceeding in this way you will efficiently foster the interests of the cognitive enterprise: the benefits will—on the whole—outweigh the costs."

Any group of mutually communicating rational inquirers is fated in the end to become a community of sorts, bound together by a shared practice or trust and cooperation, simply through self-interest operating under the evolutionary pressure of economic advantage. For when nature ("the operating environment") can be seen to function in such a way to reward a center course of action, rational people will obviously favor this course in what they do, and thereby in their teaching by example (if not also by precept).

This sort of process works on other fronts as well. Consider such operational rules as:

Be clear: Formulate your findings intelligently, avoid imprecision, equivocation, obscurity.

Be honest: Do not manipulate data, distort findings, misrepresent work.

Be careful: Do not be sloppy, indifferent to precision and exactness, heedless of pitfalls.

Be openminded: Do not ignore difficulties, neglect alternative possibilities.

Be cognitively ambitious: Strive for generality, elegance.

All such groundrules of scientific practice have been developed and consolidated because they are cost-effective within the setting of the project of inquiry. They are procedures that have as their economically cogent rationale the characteristic feature of being the cheapest (most convenient) way for us to secure the data needed for answers to our questions about the world we live in. The considerations of efficacy that lie at the root of rational selection speak loud and clear on their behalf. As one recent theorist insightfully observes:

> In science . . . the ultimate goal is not the transmission of genes but of ideas. Scientists behave as selflessly as they do because it is in their own self-interest to do so. The best thing that a scientist can do for his own career is to get his ideas accepted as his ideas by his fellow scientists. Scientists acknowledge the contribution made by other scientists because it is in their own best self-interest to do so.[8]

Rational agents are constantly impelled by the impetus of evident advantage towards a system of cooperative social practices—an operational code that serves the aims and objectives inherent in the scientific enterprise. The relevant modes of mutually helpful behavior—sharing, candor, and trustworthiness—are all strongly in everyone's interest, enabling each member to draw benefit and advantage from his own purposes. In the circumstances, cooperation emerges not necessarily from morality but even from mere self-interest. Cognitive and biological evolution alike are replete with situations in which self-interest simulates altruism—in which the course of "doing the right thing" advantages the species and the individual agent along with it.

(3) The Practices of a "Scientific Community"

The free exchange of "the scientific literature" further illustrates this state of affairs. Such an open literature initially impels the community of inquirers towards becoming a mutual assistance society and thereafter sustains it as such. Even if (contrary to fact) individual credit for one's own contributions were not forthcoming through "professional recognition," it would still be worthwhile for individuals to enter into such an arrangement. For this obviously redounds to their interests in furthering their own work—at any rate as long as intellectual curiosity is a motivating factor for them.

The commodity of information illustrates rather than contravenes the division of labor that results for Adam Smith's putative innate human "propensity to truck, barter, and exchange." The market in knowledge has pretty much the same nature and the same motivation as any other sort of market—it is a general-interest arrangement.

To be sure, it is by no means the case that the evolutionarily relevant cost-benefit advantage lies *wholly* on the side of cooperation. Competition also has its role to play. Cooperation is useful and indeed necessary in bringing budding scientists up to the frontier of current inquiry. But in moving that frontier forward—in innovation—competition has a crucial role to play.

It is illuminating in this regard to consider the reward system of science. Why do scientists, when evaluating people's contributions, accord such a great value to priority? Why make scientific discovery a "winner takes all" process, as in a political election? (After all, as long as the work was done *independently* and accomplished within the same "state of the art," the *achievement* is surely just as great?) The answer lies largely in the circumstance that this provides a maximum incentive to creative effort. Moreover, the interests of the community require avoidance of duplication of effort. The originality-promoting principle that "once done it's a dead issue" gives powerful assurance that people will not work in "dried-up" areas. The reward system of science is by and large designed to promote aims and objectives of the enterprise in the most efficient way.

This is clearly illustrated by the emergence of a reward system that apportions credit for scientific discoveries in line with their inherent importance. Good quality work is lauded to the skies and highly rewarded in "professional recognition" and other rewards while poor quality work is ignored. Such a system obviously fosters the interest of the enterprise-in-general, in which its participants all have a substantial stake. The scientific community is self-policing (to an extent that, for example, the investment industry or the medical community are not) because of mutual dependency—people are in a position where they have to make use of each other's work in the course of doing their own.

Note that even apart from the aforementioned considerations of rewards and incentives, powerful considerations of economic cost-effectiveness militate against anonymity in scientific and scholarly publication. Identification is advantageous by enabling readers to make some initial discrimination between the presumably competent work of people who, having gained good reputations through competent work, have something at risk. And their identification is clearly also a guarantor of care and conscientiousness for those who still "have to make their name" in the field. Blind publication would have the substantial disadvantage of entailing the loss of useful information. (Contemplate a scientific journal of anonymous results.)

Whether or not (and to what extent) people dedicate themselves to a certain project (medicine, science, chess playing) is indeed a social matter. But once they so do—once they seriously and dedicatedly take on such a project and its inherent teleology—then the inner mechanisms of the task situation constrain them toward the cost-effective means of the project-coordinated ends. There is then nothing accidental about their behavioral modes, for if they pursue the venture with intelligence and dedication, then rational selection will, in the course of time, inexorably bend their ways or proceed into shapes that can be accounted for in terms of economic considerations, with efficiency a major determinant of survivability.

The upshot of such deliberations is straightforward. The codes of practice by which we humans pursue the project of serious inquiry in science is the product of rational selection. The systematic practices that constitute the *modus operandi* of "the scientific community" in its various characteristic aspects are, in the main, products of a cultural evolution proceeding under the governing directive of functional effectiveness. They have emerged under the teleological pressure of purposive efficacy as the product of a fundamentally rational process of perpetuating—through acculturation, preaching, teaching, role-modeling, and the like. Just those practices flourish that are cost-effective in facilitating the efficient realization of the objectives that characterize the scientific enterprise. The factors of effectiveness and efficiency have operated to assure that the real is rational in this regard. Evolution is on the side of the economic rationality in cognitive matters not so much because it is rational as because it is economic.

NOTES

1. See, for example, P. M. Churchland, *Matter and Consciousness* (Cambridge, Mass.: MIT Press, 1984) and P. S. Churchland, *Neurophysiology: Towards a Unified Science for the Mind-Brain* (Cambridge, Mass.: MIT Press, 1986).

2. No recent writer has stressed more emphatically than F. A. Hayek the deep, inherent rationality of historical processes in contrast to the shallower calculations of a calculating intelligence that restricts its view to the agenda of the recent day. See especially his book, *The Political Order of a Free People* (Chicago, 1979), vol. 3 of *Law, Liberty, and Civilization*.

3. The French school of sociology of knowledge generally envisioned a competition among and natural/rational selection of culturally diverse modes of procedure in accounting for the evolution of logical and scientific thought. Compare Louis Rougier, *Traité de la connaisance* (Paris: Gauthier-Villans, 1955), esp. pp. 426–28.

4. C. S. Peirce, *Collected Papers*, vol. V (Cambridge, Mass.: Harvard University Press, 1934), sec. 5.366.

5. *"Im Anfang war die Tat,"* as Goethe's *Faust* puts it.

6. These present deliberations have a close kinship with the "epigenetic rules" that figure prominently in Michael Ruse's *Taking Darwin Seriously* (Oxford: Blackwell, 1986). The only significant divergence is that Ruse sees the rules at issue as having a predominantly biological basis, where the present discussion sees their basis as predominantly cultural.

7. Compare J. R. Cole and S. Cole, "The Ortega Hypothesis," *Science*, vol. 178 (1972), pp. 368–75, and also their *Social Stratifications in Science* (Chicago: University of Chicago Press, 1973).

8. David L. Hull, "Altruism in Science: A Sociobiological Model of Co-Operative Behavior Among Scientists," *Animal Behavior*, vol. 26 (1978), pp. 685–97. Hull's writings carry much grist to the mill at work in this section.

FOUR
The Intelligibility of Nature

SYNOPSIS

(1) How is the impressively effective coordination of thought and reality that is exhibited by mathematicizing natural science to be explained? Is this success perhaps simply inexplicable? Surely not! (2) To account for the cognitive accessibility of nature, a two-sided explanation is needed—one in which both our mind and external nature play a crucial collaborative role. (3) Our own side of the story lies in the fact that mind is an evolved product of nature's operations. (4) And nature's side of the story lies in its providing the stage-setting for the evolutionary development of mind. (5) Such a two-sided account can, in principle, be elaborated into a full-scale explanation that invokes the findings of science to explain how mathematicizing science itself is possible. (6) This explanation does not, however, support the overly boastful claim that "science has got it right." The critical fact is that nature must be "error tolerant" if cognitive evolution is to take place at all. And this means that one can account for the extraordinary success of natural science as we have it well short of maintaining its actual correctness.

---

(1) Explaining the Possibility of Natural Science

How is natural science—and, in particular, physics—possible at all? How is it that we insignificant humans can manage to unlock nature's secrets and gain access to her laws? And how can our mathematics—seemingly a free creative invention of the human imagination—be used so effectively to characterize the *modus operandi* of nature with such uncanny

55

efficacy and accuracy? Why is it that the majestic lawful order of nature is intelligible to us humans in our man-devised conceptual terms?[1]

As long as people thought of the world as the product of the creative activity of mathematicizing intelligence—as the work of a creator who proceeds *more mathematico* in designing nature—the issue was wholly unproblematic. God endows nature with a mathematically intelligible order and mind with a duly consonant mathematicizing intelligence. Thus, there is no problem about how the two get together—God simply arranged it that way. But, of course, if *this* is to be the canonical rationale for mind's grasp on nature's laws, then when we forego explanatory recourse to God, we also—to all appearances—lose our grip on the intelligibility of nature.

Some of the deepest intellects of the day accordingly think that this possibility is gone forever, confidently affirming that there is no way to solve this puzzle of how it is that nature is intelligible in a mathematically lawful manner. Erwin Schroedinger characterizes the circumstance that man can discover the laws of nature as "a miracle that may well be beyond human understanding."[2] Eugene Wigner asserts that "the enormous usefulness of mathematics in the natural sciences is something bordering on the mysterious, and there is no rational explanation for it"[3] and he goes on to wax surprisingly lyrical in maintaining that: "The miracle of the appropriateness of the language of mathematics for the formulation of the laws of physics is a wonderful gift which we neither understand nor deserve."[4] Even Albert Einstein stood in awe before this problem. In a letter written in 1952 to an old friend of his Berne days, Maurice Solovine, he wrote:

> You find it curious that I regard the intelligibility of the world (in the measure that we are authorized to speak of such an intelligibility) as a miracle or an eternal mystery. Well, *a priori* one should expect that the world can be rendered lawful only

to the extent that we intervene with our ordering intelligence
. . . [But] the kind of order, on the contrary, created, for
example, by Newton's theory of gravitation, is of an altogether
different character. Even if the axioms of the theory are set by
men, the success of such an endeavor presupposes in the
objective world a high degree of order that we were *a priori* in
no way authorized to expect. This is the "miracle" that is
strengthened more and more with the development of our
knowledge. . . . The curious thing is that we have to content
ourselves with recognizing the "miracle" without having a
legitimate way of going beyond it.[5]

According to all these eminent physicists, we are confronted with a profound mystery. They take the line that we
have to acknowledge *that* nature is intelligible, but we have
no prospect of understanding *why* this is so. The problem of
understanding nature's intelligibility by means of our mathematical resources is seen as intractable, unresolvable, hope-
less. All three of these distinguished Nobel laureates in
physics unblushingly employ the word "miracle" in this connection.

Perhaps, however, the question is even illegitimate and
should not be raised at all. Perhaps the issue of nature's
intelligibility is not just *intractable*, but actually *inappropriate*
and improperly based on a false presupposition. For to ask for
an explanation of *why* scientific inquiry is successful presupposes that there indeed *is* an explanatory rationale for this
fact. But if this circumstance is something fortuitous and
accidental, then, of course, no such rationale will exist at all.
Just this position is advocated by various philosophers. For
example, it is the line taken by Karl Popper, who writes:

[Traditional treatments of induction] all assume not only that
our quest for [scientific] knowledge has been successful, but
also that we should be able to explain why it is successful.
However, even on the assumption (which I share) that our

quest for knowledge has been very successful so far, and that we now know something of our universe, this success becomes [i.e., remains] miraculously improbable, and therefore inexplicable; for an appeal to an endless series of improbable accidents is not an explanation. (The best we can do, I suppose, is to investigate the almost incredible evolutionary history of these accidents . . .).[6]

Mary Hesse, too, thinks that it is inappropriate to ask for an explanation of the success of science "because science might, after all, be a miracle."[7] On this sort of view, the question of the intelligibility of nature becomes an illegitimate pseudo-problem—a forbidden fruit at which sensible minds should not presume to nibble. We must simply rest content with the fact itself, realizing that any attempt to explain it is foredoomed to failure because of the inappropriateness of the very project.

And so, on this grand question of how the success of natural science is possible at all, some of the shrewdest scientific intellects of the day avow themselves baffled, and unhesitatingly enshroud the issue in mystery or miracle.

Surely, however, such an approach has very questionable merit. Eminent authorities to the contrary notwithstanding, the question of nature's intelligibility through natural science is not only interesting and important, but is also surely one which we should, in principle, hope and expect to answer in a more or less sensible way. Clearly, this important issue needs a strong dose of demystification.

(2) A Closer Look at the Problem

How is it that we can make effective use of mathematical machinery to characterize the *modus operandi* of nature? The pure logical theorist seems to have a ready answer. He says: "Mathematics *must* apply to reality. Mathematical propositions are purely *abstract* truths whose validation turns on conceptual issues alone. Accordingly, they hold of *this* world because they hold of *every possible* world. "

But this response misses the point of present concerns. Admittedly, the truths of *pure* mathematics obtain in and of every possible world. But they do so only by virtue of the fact that they are strictly hypothetical and descriptively empty— wholly uncommitted regarding the substantive issues of the world's operations. Their very conceptual status means that the theses of pure mathematics are beside the point of our present purposes. It is not the *a priori* truth of pure mathematics that concerns us, or its ability to afford truths of reason. Rather, what is at issue is the *empirical applicability* of mathematics, its pivotal role in framing the *a posteriori*, contingent truths of lawful fact that render nature's ways amenable to reason.

After all, the fact that pure mathematics obtains in a world does not mean that this world's *laws* have to be characterizable in relatively straightforward mathematical terms. It does not mean that nature's operations have to be congenial to mathematics and graspable in terms of simple, neat, elegant, and rationally accessible formulas. In short, it does not mean that the world must be mathematically tractable and "mathematophile" in being receptive to the sort of descriptive treatment it receives in mathematical physics. How, then, are we to account for the fact that the world appears to us to be so eminently intelligible in the mathematical terms of our natural science?

The answer to this question of the cognitive accessibility of nature to mathematicizing intelligence has to lie in a somewhat complex, two-sided story in which both sides, intelligence and nature, must be expected to have a part. Let us trace out this line of thought—one step at a time.

(3)   "Our" Side

Our human side of this bilateral story is relatively straight-forward. After all, *homo sapiens* is an integral part of nature. We are connected into nature's scheme of things as an intrinsic component thereof—courtesy of the processes of evolution. Our experience is thus inevitably an experience *of nature*. (That after all is what "experience" is—our intelligence-mediated reaction to the world's stimulating impacts upon us.) So the kind of mathematics—the kind of theory of periodicity and structure—that we devise in the light of this experience is the kind that is, in principle, applicable to nature as we can experience it. As C. S. Peirce insisted, evolutionary pressures conform our intellectual processes to the *modus operandi* of nature. For nature not only *teaches* us (when we chose to study it) but also *forms* us (whether or not we chose to study it). And it proceeds in doing the latter in a way that is not, and cannot be, without implications for the former.

Our mathematics is destined to be attuned to nature because it itself is a natural product as a thought-instrument of ours: it fits nature because it reflects the way we ourselves are emplaced within nature as integral constituents thereof. Our intellectual mechanisms—mathematics included—fit nature because they are themselves a product of nature's operations as mediated through the cognitive processes of an intelligent creature that uses its intelligence to guide its interaction with a nature into which it is itself fitted in a particular sort of way.

It should be recognized that the mathematics of an astronomically remote civilization whose experiential resources differ from ours might well be substantially different from mathematics as we ourselves know it. Their dealings with collective manifolds might be entirely anumerical—purely comparative, for example, rather than quantitative, especially if their environment is not amply endowed with solid objects or stable structures congenial to measurement. If, for example they were jellyfish-like creatures swimming about in a soupy sea, their "geometry" could be something rather strange, largely topological, say, and geared to flexible structures rather than to fixed sizes or shapes. Digital thinking might go undeveloped while certain sorts of analogue reasoning might be highly refined. In particular, if the intelligent aliens were a diffuse assemblage of units that constitute wholes in ways permitting overlap, then social concepts might become so paramount in their thinking that nature would throughout be viewed in fundamentally social categories, with those aggregates we think of as *physical* structures contemplated by them in *social* terms. Communicating by some sort of "telepathy" based upon variable odors or otherwise "exotic" signals, they might, for example, devise a complex theory of empathetic thought-wave transmittal through an ideaferous aether. The processes that underlie their mathematicizing might be very different indeed.

Admittedly, mathematics is not a natural science but a theory of hypothetical possibilities. Nevertheless, these possibilities are possibilities as conceived by beings who do their possibility-conceiving with a nature-evolved and nature-implanted mind. It is thus not surprising that the sort of mathematics we contrive is the sort of mathematics we find applicable to the conceptualization of nature. After all, the intellectual mechanisms we devise in coming to grips with the world—in transmuting sensory interaction with nature into intelligible experience—have themselves the aspect (among many other aspects) of being nature's contrivances in adjusting to its ways a creature it holds at its mercy.

It is no more a miracle that the human mind can understand the world through its conceptual resources than that the human eye can see it through its physiological resources. The critical step is to recognize that the question "Why do our conceptual methods and mechanisms fit 'the real world' with which we interact intellectually?" is to be answered in basically the same way as the question: "Why do our bodily processes and mechanisms fit the world with which we interact physically?" In neither case can we proceed in terms of purely theoretical grounds of general principle. Both issues are alike to be resolved in essentially evolutionary terms. It is no more surprising that our minds grasp nature's ways than it is surprising that our eyes can accommodate nature's rays or our stomachs nature's food. As we have noted from the outset, evolutionary pressures can take credit for the lot: they are part and parcel of what is mandated by attainment to our niche in nature's scheme of things. There is nothing "miraculous" or "lucky" in our possession of efficient cognitive faculties and processes—effective "hardware" and "software" for productive inquiry. If we did not possess such capacities, we just wouldn't be here as inquiring creatures emplaced in nature by evolutionary processes.

Moreover, intelligent beings that arise through evolution are bound to deem their world to be mathematically elegant if they press their inquiries in the right direction. For the very self-same forces that are at work in shaping physical nature are also at work in shaping our bodies and brains and in providing the stimuli that impinge on our senses and our minds. It is these interactions between thought and world that condition our sense of order and beauty—of regularity, symmetry, economy, and elegance. The modes of order that attract the attention of mathematical theorists interested in structures—the concepts that shape their ideas of beautiful theories—are thus, unsurprisingly, also at work in the nature within which these conceptualizations arise. Evolutionary pressure coordinates the mind with its environment. Even as we are destined to find healthy foods palatable and reproductively advantageous activities pleasant, so nature's inherent order and structure are bound to prove congenial to our mathematical sense of elegance and beauty. The mathematical mechanisms we employ for understanding the standard features of things themselves reflect the structure of our *experience*.

Nevertheless, it could perhaps be the case that we succeed in mathematicizing nature only as regards the immediate local microenvironment that defines our particular limited ecological niche. The possibility still remains open that we secure our cognitive hold on only a small and peripheral part of a large and impenetrable whole. And so, man's own one-sided contribution to the matter of nature's intelligibility cannot be the *whole* story regarding the success of science. For even if we do reasonably well in regard to our own immediate evolutionary requirements, this might still be very inadequate in the larger scheme of things. Nature's receptiveness to our cognitive efforts remains to be accounted for—the fact that nature is *substantially* amenable to reason and not just *somewhat* (and perhaps only very marginally) so.

To clarify this issue we must therefore move on to consider nature's contribution to the bilateral mind/nature relationship.

(4) Nature's Side

What needs to be explained for present purposes is why mathematics is not merely of *some* utility in understanding the world, but actually of *very substantial* utility—that its employment can provide intelligent inquirers with an adequate and accurate grasp of nature's ways. We must thus probe more deeply into the issue of nature's amenability to inquiry and its accessibility to the probes of intelligence.

To be sure, the effective applicability of mathematics to the description of nature is in no small part due to the fact that we actually devise our mathematics to fit nature through the mediation of experience. But the fact remains that if an inquiring being, who is emplaced within nature and forms his mathematicized conceptions and beliefs about it on the basis of physical interaction with it, is to achieve a reasonably appropriate grasp of its workings, then nature too must "do its part"—it must be duly cooperative. Given the supposition at issue, it must, obviously, permit the evolution of inquiring beings. And to do this, it must present them with an environment that affords sufficiently stable patterns to make coherent "experience" possible, enabling them to derive appropriate *information* from those structured interactions that prevail in nature at large. Nature's own contribution to the mathematical intelligibility of nature must accordingly be the possession of a relatively simple and uniform law structure—one that deploys so uncomplicated a set of regularities that even a community of inquirers possessed of only rather moderate capabilities can be expected to achieve a fairly good grasp of the processes at work in their environment.

But how can one establish that—relative to our suppositions—nature simply *"must"* have a fairly straightforward law structure? Are there any fundamental reasons why the world that we investigate by the use of our mathematically informed intelligence should operate on relatively simple principles that are readily amenable to mathematical characterization?

There are indeed. For a world in which intelligence emerges by anything like standard *evolutionary* processes has to be pervaded by regularities and periodicities in the organism-nature interaction that produces and perpetuates organic species. And this means that nature must be cooperative in a certain very particular way; it must be stable enough and regular enough and structured enough for there to be appropriate responses to natural events that can be "learned" by creatures. If such "appropriate responses" are to develop, nature must provide suitable stimuli in a duly structured way. An organically viable environment—to say nothing of a *knowable* one—must incorporate experientiable structures.

There must be regular patterns of occurrence in nature that even simple, single-celled creatures can embody in their make-up and reflect in their *modus operandi*. Even the humblest organisms, snails, say, and even algae, must so operate so that certain *types of stimuli* (patterns of recurrently discernible impacts) call forth appropriately corresponding *types of response*, so that such organisms can "detect" a structured pattern in their natural environment and react to it in a way that proves to their advantage in evolutionary terms. Even nature's simplest creatures can maintain themselves in existence only by swimming in a sea of detectable regularities of a sort that will be readily accessible to intelligence. Their world must encapsulate straightforwardly "learnable" patterns and periodicities of occurrence in its operations—in other words, relatively simple laws.

Accordingly, a world in which intelligence can develop by evolutionary processes *must* also—on this basis—be a world amenable to understanding in mathematical terms.[8] It must be a world whose cognizing beings will find much grist to their mill in endeavoring to "understand" the world. Galileo long ago hit close to the mark when he wrote in his *Dialogues* that "Nature initially arranged things her *own* way and subsequently so constructed the human intellect as to be able to understand her."[9] But of course nature's construction of mathematicizing mind has proceeded by evolutionary processes.

The development of *life* and thereafter of *intelligence* in the world may or may not be inevitable; the emergence of intelligent creatures on the world's stage may or may not be surprising in itself and as such. But once they are there, and once we realize that they got there thanks to evolutionary processes, it can no longer be seen as surprising that their efforts at characterizing the world in mathematical terms should be substantially successful. *A world in which intelligent creatures emerge through the operation of evolutionary processes must be an intelligible world.*

On this line of deliberation, then, nature admits of mathematical depiction not just because it has laws—is a *cosmos*—but because as an evolution-permitting world it must have many *relatively simple* laws. And those relatively simple laws must be there because if they were not, then nature just would not afford the sort of environmental requisite for the evolutionary development of intelligent life. An intelligence-containing world whose intelligent creatures came by this intelligence through evolutionary means must be substantially intelligible in mathematical terms.

The apparent success of human mathematics in characterizing nature is thus nowise amazing. It may or may not call for wonder that intelligent creatures should evolve at all. But thereupon, once they have safely arrived on the scene through evolutionary means, it is only natural and to be expected that they should be able to achieve success in the project of understanding nature in mathematical terms. A mathematicizing intelligence *arrived at through evolution* must for this very reason prove to be substantially successful in alignment with the world's ways.

The strictly hypothetical and conditional character of this general line of reasoning must be recognized. It does not maintain that by virtue of some sort of transcendental necessity the world has to be simple enough for its mode of operation to admit of elegant mathematical representation. Rather, what it maintains is the purely conditional thesis that *if* intelligent creatures are going to emerge in the world by evolutionary processes, *then* the world must be mathematophile, with various of its processes amenable to mathematical representation.

It must be stressed, however, that this conditional fact is quite sufficient for present purposes. For the question we face is why we intelligent creatures present on the world's stage should be able to understand its operations in terms of our mathematics. The conditional story at issue fully suffices to accomplish this particular job.

One brief digression to avert a possible misunderstanding is in order. Nothing whatever in our argumentation can properly be construed to claim that the development of mathematics is an evolutionary requirement or desideratum as such—that creatures are somehow impelled to develop mathematics because it advantages them in the struggle for existence. (This idea would be a foolish anachronism, seeing that evolution produced man milennia before man produced mathematics.) All that is being maintained is: (1) that intelligence is (in certain circumstances) of evolutionary advantage; (2) that any sufficiently intelligent creature *can* develop a mathematics (a theory of structure); and (3) that any sufficiently intelligent creature must be able to develop a "mathematics" of sorts in any world able to give rise to it through evolutionary means. To say that *intelligence,* the precondition of mathematics, is of evolutionary advantage, is not to claim that this is the case with mathematics itself.

(5) Synthesis

A brief review of the results of the preceding deliberations is in order.

The overall question of the intelligibility of nature has two sides:

I. Why is mind so well attuned to nature?

II. Why is nature so well attuned to mind?

The preceding discussion has suggested that the answers to these questions are not all that complicated—at least at the level of schematic essentials. The crux is simply this: mind must be attuned to nature since intelligence is a generalized guide to conduct that has evolved as a natural product of nature's operations. And nature must be accessible to mind if intelligence manages to evolve within nature by a specifically evolutionary route.

For nature to be intelligible, then, there must be an alignment that requires cooperation on both sides. The analogy of cryptanalysis is suggestive. If A is to break B's code, there must be due reciprocal alignment. If A's methods are too crude, too hit and miss, he can get nowhere. But even if A is quite intelligent and resourceful, his efforts cannot succeed if B's procedures are simply beyond his powers. (The cryptanalysts of the seventeenth century, clever though they were, could get absolutely nowhere in applying their investigative instrumentalities to a high-level naval code of World War II vintage.) Analogously, if mind and nature were too far out of alignment—if mind were too "unintelligent" for the complexities of nature or nature too complex for the capacities of mind, the two just couldn't get into step. It would be like trying to rewrite Shakespeare in a pidgin English with a five-hundred word vocabulary or trying to monitor the workings of a system with ten degrees of freedom by using a cognitive mechanism capable of keeping track of four of them. If something like this were the case, mind could not accomplish its evolutionary mission. It would be better to adopt an alignment process that doesn't take the cognitive route. Just as any creature that evolves in nature must find due physical accommodation within it (a due harmonization of its bodily operations and its material environs), so any mind that evolves in nature must find due intellectual accommodation within it (a due harmonization of its intellectual operations with its structural environs). In consequence, there must be a due equilibration between the mind's mathematizing operations and the world's mathematical structure.

The solution of our problem accordingly roots in the combination of two considerations: (1) a world that admits of the evolutionary emergence of intelligence must be (relatively) regular and simple, i.e., must be mathematophile; and

(2) a sufficiently powerful intelligence must be able to effectively comprehend in mathematical terms any world in which it gains its foothold by evolutionary means. The possibility of a mathematical science of nature is, accordingly, to be explained by the fact that, in the light of evolution, intelligence and intelligibility must stand in mutual coordination.

Three points are accordingly paramount here:

1. Intelligence evolves within a nature that provides for life because it affords living creatures a good way of coming to terms with the world;

2. Once intelligent creatures evolve, their cognitive efforts are likely to have some degree of adequacy because evolutionary pressures align them with nature's ways;

3. It should not be surprising that this alignment eventually produces a substantially effective mathematical physics, because the structure of the operations of a nature that engenders intelligence by an evolutionary route is bound to be relatively simple.

No doubt, this somewhat schematic account requires much amplification and concretization. A long and complex tale must be told about physical and cognitive evolution to fill in the details needed to put such an account into a properly compelling form. But there is surely good reason to hope and expect that a tale of this sort can ultimately be told.

And this is the pivotal point. Even if one has doubts about the particular outlines of the evolutionary story we have sketched, the fact remains that *some such story* can provide a perfectly workable answer to the question of why nature's ways are intelligible to us in terms of our mathematical instrumentalities. The mere fact that such an account is in principle possible shows that the issue need not be painted in the black on black of impenetrable mystery.

There may indeed be mysteries in this general area. Questions like "Why should it be that *life* evolves in the world?" and, even more fundamentally, "Why should it be that the world exists at all?" may plausibly be proposed as candidates. But be that as it may, the presently deliberated issue of why nature is intelligible to us, and why this intelligibility should incorporate a mathematically articulable physics, does not qualify as all that mysterious, let alone miraculous.

There is simply no need to join Einstein, Schroedinger, and others in considering the intelligibility of nature as a miracle or a mystery that passes all human understanding. If we are willing to learn from science itself how nature operates and how man goes about conducting his inquiries into its workings, then we should increasingly be able to remove the shadow of incomprehension from the problem of how it is that a being of *this* sort, probing an environment of *that* type, and doing so by means of *those* particular evolutionary developed cognitive and physical instrumentalities, manages to arrive at a relatively workable account of how things work in the world. We should eventually be able to see it as only plausible and to be expected that inquiring beings should emerge in nature and get themselves into a position to make a relatively good job of coming to comprehend it. We can thus *look to science itself* for the materials that enable us to understand how natural science is possible. There is no good reason to expect that it will let us down in this regard.[10]

Admittedly, any such scientifically informed account of science's ability to understand the world is, in a way, circular. It explains the possibility of our knowledge of nature on the basis of what we know of nature's ways. Its explanatory strategy uses the deliverances of natural science retrospectively to provide an account of how an effective natural science is possible. Such a procedure is *not*, however, a matter of vitiating circularity, but one of the healthy and virtuous self-sufficiency of our knowledge that is, in fact, an essential part of its claims to adequacy.[11] Any scientific world-picture that does not provide materials for explaining the success of science itself would thereby manifest a failing in its grasp of the phenomena of nature that betokens its own inadequacy.[12]

Implications

But does such a scientific explanation of the success of science not explain too much? Will its account of the pervasiveness of mathematical exactness in science not lead to the (obviously problematic) consequence that "science gets it right"—a result that would fly in the face of our historical experience of science's fallibilism?

By no means! It is fortunate (and evolutionarily most relevant) that we are so positioned within nature that many "wrong" paths lead to the "right" destination, that flawed means often lead us to cognitively satisfactory ends. If nature were a combination lock where we simply "had to get it right"— and *exactly* right—to achieve success in implementing our beliefs, then we just wouldn't be here. Evolution is not an argument that speaks unequivocally for the adequacy of our cognitive efforts. On the contrary, properly construed it is an indicator of our capacity to err and "get away with it." Admittedly, applicative success calls for *some* alignment of thought-governed action with "the real *nature* of things," but only enough to get by without incurring overly serious penalties in failure.

The success of science should be understood somewhat on analogy with the success of the thirsty man who drank white grape juice, mistaking it for lemonade. It is not that he was roughly right—that such grape juice is "approximately" lemonade. It's just that his beliefs are not wrong in ways that lead us to his being baffled in his present purposes—that such defects as they have do not matter for the issues currently in hand. The "success" at issue is doubtless not unqualified but mixed, though in the circumstances, we cannot help laboring under the impression that our science is very successful. It follows that intelligence and the "science" it devises must pay off in terms of applicative success—irrespective of whether it manages to get things substantially right or not.

Accordingly, the applicative success of our science is not to be explained on the basis of its actually getting at the real truth, but in terms of its being the work of a cognitive being who operates within an error-tolerant environment—a world-setting where applicative success will attend even theories that are substantially "off the mark." The applicative efficacy of science undoubtedly requires *some* degree of alignment between our world-picture and the world's actual arrangements—but only just enough to yield the particular successes at issue. No claims to finality or perfection can therefore be substantiated for our science as it stands here and now.

We thus arrive at the picture of nature as an error-tolerant system. For consider the hypothetical situation of a species of belief-guided creatures living in an environment that invariably exacts a great penalty for "getting it wrong." Whenever the creature makes the smallest mistake—the least little cognitive misstep—bang, it's dead! Our hypothesis is not viable: any such creature would have been eliminated long ago. It could not even manage to survive and reproduce long enough to learn about its environment by trial and error. If the world is to be a home for intelligent beings who develop in it through evolution, then it has to be benign: it has to be error-tolerant. For if nature were not error-forgiving, a process of evolutionary trial and error could not work, and intelligent organisms could not emerge at all.[13]

Evolution is indeed the guarantor of a reciprocal attunement of mind and nature, but it by no means requires that this attunement be of a very high grade. It is one thing to be right and another to be so badly wrong that one is baffled of one's purposes. This sort of functional adequacy is something very different from truth. Such a perspective indicates that the success of the applications of our current science does not betoken its actual truth, but merely means that those ways (whatever they be) in which it fails to be true are immaterial to the achievement of success, that in the context of the particular applications at issue its inadequacies lie beneath the penalty threshold of failure.

Accordingly, the success of science can be explained well short of the supposition that it manages to get at the real truth of nature's arrangements. The success of our natural science does not betoken its correctness, seeing that evolution requires an "error-tolerant" nature that can afford success despite falsity. If *seeming* success in intellectually governed operations could not attend even substantially erroneous beliefs, then we cognizing beings who have to learn by experience—by trial and error—just couldn't have made our way along the corridor of time. This critical fact that evolution requires an error-tolerant environment means that we can explain the impressive successes of mathematicizing natural science without making untenable claims as to its definitive correctness.

NOTES

1. This very Kantian issue will here be treated in a very un-Kantian way, for the present deliberations will not invoke, as with Kant, certain *a priori* principles that supposedly *underlie* physics. Rather, our tale will unfold in terms of the factual (*a posteriori*) principles that *constitute* physics—the putative laws of nature themselves.

2. Erwin Schroedinger, *What is Life?* (Cambridge: University of Cambridge Press, 1945), p. 31.

3. Eugene P. Wigner, "The Unreasonable Effectiveness of Mathematics in the Natural Sciences," *Communications on Pure and Applied Mathematics*, vol. 13 (1960), pp. 1–14 (see p. 2).

4. *Ibid.*, p. 14.

5. Albert Einstein, *Lettres à Maurice Solovine* (Paris: Gauthier-Villars, 1956), pp. 114–15.

6. K. R. Popper, *Objective Knowledge* (Oxford: Clarendon Press, 1972), p. 28.

7. Mary Hesse, *Revolutions and Reconstructions in the Philosophy of Science* (Bloomington: University of Illinois Press, 1980), p. 154.

8. Conversations with Gerald Massey have helped to clarify this part of the argument.

9. Galileo Galilei, *Dialogo II in Le Opere di Galileo Galilei* (Edizio Nazionale, vols. I–XX, Florence, 1890–1909). vol VII, p. 298. (I owe this reference to Juergen Mittelstrass.) Kepler wrote, "Thus God himself was too kind to remain idle, and began to play the game of signatures, signing his likeness into the world. I therefore venture to think that all nature and all the graceful sky are symbolized in the art of geometry." Quoted in Freeman Dyson, "Mathematics in the Physical Sciences," in *The Mathematical Sciences*, ed. by the Committee on Support of Research in the Mathematical Sciences (Cambridge, Mass: Harvard University Press, 1969), p. 99.

10. The preceding account draws upon the author's *The Riddle of Existence* (Lanham: University Press of America, 1984).

11. Just this approach is the salient feature of W.V.O. Quine's program of "Epistemology Naturalized:" "Our question, 'Why is science so successful?' [is to be] taken . . . as a scientific question, open to investigation by natural science itself. . . . Individuals whose similarity groupings conduce largely to true expectations have a good chance of finding food and avoiding predators, and so a good chance of living to reproduce their kind. . . . I am not appealing to Darwinian biology to justify induction. This would be circular, since biological knowledge depends upon induction, and then observing that Darwinian biology, if true, helps explain why induction is so efficacious as it is." (W.V.O. Quine, "The Nature of Natural Knowledge," in *Mind and Language*, ed. by S. Gutemplan [Oxford, 1975], pp. 67–81; see p. 70). My only reservation about this sensible passage relates to Quine's feeling of a need to apologize for using the *products* of induction in the course of justifying the *use* of induction. Rather complex argumentation can show that such a procedure can, in suitable circumstances, not only not be vicious but even appropriate. See Gerhard Vollmer, "On Supposed Circularities in an

Empirically Oriented Epistemology" in G. Radnitzky *et al.*, *Evolutionary Epistemology* (La Salle, Ill.: Open Court, 1987), pp. 163–200. What is at issue is only a matter of getting a suitable starting point, even as we use a product of nutrition, namely energy, to carry on the process of nutrition itself. See also the author's *Scepticism* (Oxford: Blackwell, 1980).

12. Some of the ideas of this discussion are developed more fully in the author's *Scientific Realism* (Dordrecht: Reidel, 1987).

13. It is this unavoidable error-tolerant aspect of nature that blocks any prospect of a naive "it works, therefore it's true" pragmatism at the level of individual *theses*. But the situation is different, as regards large-scale *methods* from providing action-guiding theses. Here "it works, therefore it's cogent (as an inquiry method, i.e. its deliverances are actually credible)" is something else again. See the author's *Methodological Pragmatism* (Oxford: Blackwell, 1977).

FIVE

Our Science as O-U-R Science

SYNOPSIS

(1) Natural science does not depict "reality as such," but rather afford us a picture of "reality as it presents itself to us"—we being inquirers of a certain particular sort, with a certain particular, evolution-determined mode of emplacement in the world's scheme of things. Our scientific picture of nature is the product of an interaction in which both parties—we investigators and nature herself—make a crucial *and inseparable* contribution. (2) The inquiring intelligences of an extraterrestrial civilization might also develop a science. (3) But this would not necessarily be anything like our science. While dealing with the same world, it would doubtless differ in mode of formulation, in subject-matter orientation, and in conceptualization. (4) The one-world one-science argument is ultimately untenable. Natural science as we have it is a human artifact that is bound to be limited in crucial respects by the very fact of its being *our* science. (5) The world-as-we-know-it is accordingly *our* world—the correlate of mind of a world-picture devised in characteristically human terms of reference. Being the product of our *experience* of nature, our empirical science is bound to reflect, at least in part, the peculiar character of our evolutionary heritage. (6) This perspective does not *deny* realism, but *relativizes* it to our place in nature. It does not gainsay the existence of a "mind-independent reality," but insists that our *view* of this reality is always mediated through conceptions that reflect how this reality affects us.

(1) Scientific Relativism

There is no adequate reason of general principle for thinking of our own human scientific view of the world as cognitively absolute, devoid of relativization to the character of the two-sidedly collaborative interaction that obtains between the world and its investigators. We must recognize that, even in cognition, process and product are reciprocally interwoven—that our scientific picture of nature is the product of an *interaction* in which both parties, both nature and ourselves, make a formative contribution. The result of our investigations of nature is, accordingly, something in whose overall constitution the respective inputs of the two parties simply cannot be separated from one another—at any rate not by us.

The query "What is the discoverable character of nature—what are the detectable *components* of physical reality, and what are the discernible *regularities* that govern them?" remains incomplete and defective unless we first resolve the question: "Detectable and discernible *by whom?*" For the issue is one that is inevitably relativized to the nature-interactive resources and instrumentalities at the disposal of investigators.

To be sure, the regularities of nature are something perfectly real and independent of the wants and wishes of inquirers. But nevertheless, their reality is a *relational* reality—a matter of interaction between the world and its investigators. We must, accordingly, regard our knowledge of the world as being, in inseparable part, a function of the manner of our evolutionary attunement to nature.

Factual (empirically based) theses regarding how things work in the world are always correlative with the issue of monitoring, of interaction/detection, of what can be "perceived" about nature from the vantage point of being emplaced therein and equipped with certain facilities for interaction with it. And this circumstance underwrites a certain sort of scientific relativism. For science is a matter of explaining "how things work" in the world. We can explain only what we can discern because our facilities for discernment reflect our mode of emplacement within nature. This inevitably conditions even the kinds of scientific issues we can address, relativizing them in part to the character of our evolved enmeshment in nature's scheme of things.

The regularities of nature that can be discovered by *us* depends on who *we* are. Our reality (reality as *we* know it) is something whose nature is relativized to us humans—which is, of course, true of other cognizing beings as well. Reality-as-we-know-it is something relational, though of course reality as such is not. (The range of *fact* is always broader than that of *knowledge*.)

Consider an analogy. Some oil makes a slick on a pool of water, twisting about on the rippling surface. Suppose someone asks: "What is the shape (or configuration) of that oil as such—in itself and without reference to the water on which it is emplaced?" We are baffled. What answer can one possibly give? The only shape there is is that interactive configuration in whose make-up the role of the water is every bit as determinative as the oil itself. The relative contributions of the two parties simply cannot be separated. Analogously, the "shape of our knowledge" in natural science is something interactive that hinges every bit as much on the evolved medium of their emplacement as on the constitution of the objects themselves. Science furnishes appropriate information about the world all right, but information that is "appropriate" from our own cognitive point of view. Our empirical inquiries do not afford us a picture of "reality in itself," but rather as a matter of "reality as it presents itself to us inquirers of a certain particular sort." Natural science is, in an important sense, *our* science, and it describes reality not in a categorical and absolute way, but by providing investigator-relative results that differ with different modes of interaction between investigators and their natural environment.

On such a view, inquiry yields results that are inherently relational. This does not mean that there is no such thing as a self-subsistingly nonrelational reality. Rather, it means that reality *"as we picture it"* is a complex composite in whose constitution we ourselves play an uneliminable role through the particular characteristic of our evolutionary attunement to nature.

To say all this is not to espouse scepticism and deny the attainability of duly evidentiated information about the world. Instead, it is to accept a (realistic) mode of relationalism—to recognize that the *modus operandi* of investigators always crucially condition the sort of information that their science is in a position to provide about the world. One's situation in point of data-accessibility and information-processing capacities is bound to condition the scientific world-picture at which one will arrive.

What is brought into question from this perspective is not the *existence* of "the real world" that is self-subsistingly mind-independent, but the *status of our knowledge* of it. For it emerges that the *knowledge* of ("mind-independent") reality is not itself mind-independent, but represents information about an inquiry-relative *empirical* reality. We arrive at the position that our knowledge of the world is developed from the characteristically human perspective in the overall disposition of things in nature and affords a view of reality as experientially accessible "from the human point of view." It is species-relativized because the reality with which it deals is *our* reality—nature as our own particular evolutionary heritage cognitive instrumentalities reveals it to us.[1]

(2) The Problem of Extraterrestrial Science

But is natural science not something altogether investigator-independent—a body of self-subsistent fact, wholly disconnected from the proceedings of its practitioners, something that represents a destination that all (sufficiently clever) inquiring intelligences are bound ultimately to reach in common?

To elucidate this idea of investigator convergence, let us consider the prospect that a civilization of extraterrestrial aliens, living on a planet in some far-off galaxy, might also develop natural science and its concomitant technology.[2]

This seemingly simple assumption is, in fact, one of great complexity; and this complexity relates not only to the actual or possible facts of the matter, but also—and crucially—to fundamental questions about the very idea that is at issue here.

First off, there is the matter of just what it means for there to be another science-possessing civilization. Note that this is a question that *we* are putting—a question posed in terms of the applicability of *our* term "science." It pivots on the issue of whether *we* would be prepared to recognize what those aliens are doing as a matter of forming beliefs (theories) about how things work in the world and to acknowledge that they are involved in testing these beliefs observationally or experimentally and in applying them in practical (technological) contexts. We must be prepared to accept those alien creatures as (non-human) *persons* duly equipped with intellect and will, and thereupon embark on a complex series of claims with respect to their cognitive activities.

A scientific civilization is not merely one that possesses intelligence and social organization, but one that puts this intelligence and organization to work in a very particular way. This opens up a rather subtle issue of priority in regard to process versus product. Is the requisite for a civilization's "having a science" primarily a matter of the substantive *content* of their doctrines (their belief structures and theory complexes), or is it primarily a matter of the *aims and purposes* with a view to which their doctrines are formed (control, prediction, explanation, and the like)?

The issue of content turns on how similar their scientific beliefs are to ours, which is clearly something in which we would be ill-advised to put much stock. After all, the speculations of the nature-theorists of preSocratic Greece, our ultimate predecessors in the scientific enterprise, bear precious little *substantive* resemblance to our present-day sciences, nor does the content of contemporary physics bear all that much resemblance to that of Newton's day. In adjudging scientific status, we would do better to give prime emphasis to matters of process and purpose rather than products and results.

Accordingly, the matter of these aliens "having a science" should be seen as turning not on the extent to which their *findings* resemble ours, but on the extent to which their *projects* resemble ours. The crux is whether we are engaged in the same sort of rational inquiry in terms of the sorts of issues being addressed and the ways in which they are going about addressing them. The issue is, at bottom, not one of the *substantive similarity* of their "science" to ours, but one of the *functional equivalency* of their projects to the scientific enterprise as we know it. Only if they are pursuing such goals as description, explanation, prediction, and control of nature will they be doing *science*.

This perspective has far-reaching implications.

(3) The Potential Diversity of "Science"

It is illuminating to approach the problems of different "sciences" from the angle of the question: To what extent would the *functional equivalent* of natural science built up by the inquiring intelligences of an astronomically remote civilization be bound to resemble our science? In reflecting on this question and its ramifications, one soon comes to realize that there is an enormous potential for diversity.

For one thing, the *orientation* of the science of an alien civilization might be altogether different. All their efforts might conceivably be devoted to the social science—to developing highly sophisticated analogues of psychology and sociology, for example. In particular, if the intelligent aliens were a diffuse assemblage of units constituting wholes in ways that allow of overlap,[3] then the role of social concepts might become so paramount for them that nature would throughout be viewed in fundamentally social categories, with those aggregates that we think of as physical structures contemplated by them in social terms. Accordingly, their natural science might deploy explanatory mechanisms very different from ours. Communicating by some sort of "telepathy" based upon variable odors of otherwise "exotic" signals, they might devise a complex theory of empathetic thought-wave transmittal through an ideaferous aether.

Again, the aliens might scan nature very differently. Electromagnetic phenomena might lie wholly outside the ken of variant life-forms; if their environment does not afford them lodestones and electrical storms, the occasion to develop electromagnetic theory might never arise. The course of scientific development tends to flow in the channel of practical interests. A society of porpoises will probably lack crystallography but may develop a very sophisticated hydrodynamics. Similarly, mole-like creatures might never dream of developing optics or astronomy. One's language and thought processes are bound to be closely geared to the world as one experiences it, as is illustrated by the difficulties we ourselves have in bringing the language of everyday experience to bear on subatomic phenomena (our concepts are ill-attuned to facets of nature different in scale or structure from our own). We can hardly expect a "science" that reflects such parochial preoccupations to be a universal fixture. The interests of creatures shaped under the remorseless pressure of evolutionary adaptions to very different—and endlessly variable—environmental conditions will doubtless be oriented in directions very different from anything familiar to us.

Laws are detectable regularities in nature. But detection, of course, varies drastically with the mode of observation—that is, with the sort of resources that different creatures have at their disposal to do their detecting. Everything depends on how nature impacts upon a creature's senses and their instrumental extensions. Even if we were to discern everything that we can manage to detect, we would still be very far from having got hold of everything available to others (and the reverse is equally true). Since the laws we find are bound to reflect the sorts of data we can get hold of, the laws that we (or anybody else) can manage to formulate will depend crucially on one's place within nature—on how one is connected into its wiring diagram, so to speak.

Supporting considerations for this position have been advanced from very different points of view. One example is a thought experiment suggested by Georg Simmel in the last century that envisaged an entirely different sort of cognitive being: intelligent and actively inquiring creatures (animals, say, or beings from outer space) whose experiential modes differ substantially from ours.[4] Their senses respond rather differently to physical influences: they are relatively insensitive, say, to heat and light, but substantially sensitized to various electromagnetic phenomena. Such intelligent creatures, Simmel held, could plausibly be supposed to operate within a significantly variant framework of empirical concepts and categories; the events and objects of the world of their experience might be radically distinct from those of our own: their phenomenological predicates, for example, might have altogether variant descriptive domains. In a similar vein, William James wrote:

> Were we lobsters, or bees, it might be that our organization would have led to our using quite different modes from these [actual ones] of apprehending our experiences. It *might* be too (we cannot dogmatically deny this) that such categories uni-

maginable by us to-day, would have proved on the whole as serviceable for handling our experiences mentally as those we actually use.[5]

The science of a different civilization would inevitably be closely tied to the particular pattern of their interaction with nature as funneled through the particular course of their evolutionary adjustment to their specific environment. The "forms of sensibility" of radically different beings (to invoke Kant's useful idea) are likely to be radically diverse from ours. The direct chemical analysis of environmental materials might prove highly useful, and bioanalytic techniques akin to our senses of taste and smell could be very highly developed, providing them with "experiences" of their chemical environment of a sort very different from ours.

Moreover, the *conceptualization* of an alien science might also be very different. For we must also reckon with the possibility that a remote civilization might operate with a drastically different system of concepts in its cognitive dealings with nature. Different cultures and different intellectual traditions, to say nothing of different sorts of creatures, are bound to describe and explain their experience—their world as they conceive it—in terms of concepts and categories of understanding substantially different from ours. They would diverge radically with respect to what the Germans call their *Denkmittel*—the conceptual instruments they employ in thinking about the facts (or purported facts) of the world. They could, accordingly, be said to operate with different conceptual schemes, with different ideational tools used to "make sense" of experience—to characterize, describe, and explain the items that figure in the world as they view it. The taxonomic and explanatory mechanisms by means of which their cognitive business is transacted could differ so radically from ours that intellectual contact with them would be difficult or impossible.

To clarify this position, consider the analogy between *perception* and *conception*. It is clear that there is no single "uniquely correct and appropriate" mode of perception. Different sorts of creatures have very different sorts of senses, and perceive the world very differently by their means. The situation with conception is, in many ways, similar to this. Conceptualization too can clearly be done in very different ways. To be sure, there is also an important disanalogy. Conception lets us step beyond the domain of our perception and enables us, as human scientists, to describe how very different sorts of creatures can sense the world—i.e. how they go about monitoring their environment in physical interaction in ways different from ours. We can represent their *sensory* framework within our *conceptual* framework. But this we cannot do with conception itself. There is no supraconceptual vantage point from which *we* (at any rate) can compare and contrast how different sorts of creatures might conceive the world differently from ourselves. It is a near-trivial truth, but for that very reason still a truth, that we ourselves must inevitably understand *any* sort of concepts in terms of *our* concepts. (Once we appropriate concepts, we *ipso facto* make them ours.) But this disanalogy just strengthens the point at issue—namely, that there is nothing necessarily definitive about *our* way of conceptualizing the world and that we have no choice but to accept that different sorts of creatures could manage the matter very differently.

A comparison of the "science" of different civilizations here on earth suggests that it is not an outlandish hypothesis to suppose that the very *topics* of alien science might differ dramatically from those of ours. In our own case, for example, the fact that we live on the surface of the earth (unlike whales), the fact that we have eyes (unlike worms) and thus can *see* the heavens, the fact that we are so situated that the seasonal positions of heavenly bodies are intricately connected with agriculture—all these facts are clearly connected with the development of astronomy. The fact that those distant creatures would experience nature in ways radically different from ourselves means that they can be expected to raise very different sorts of questions. Indeed, the mode of emplacement within nature of alien inquirers might be so different as to focus their attention on entirely different aspects or constituents of the cosmos. If the world is sufficiently complex and multifaceted, they might concentrate upon aspects of their environment that mean nothing to us, with the result that their natural science is oriented in directions very different from ours.[6]

Epistemologists often insist that people whose experience of the world differs substantially from our own are bound to conceive of it in very different terms. Sociologists, anthropologists, and linguists talk in much the same way, and philosophers of science have recently also come to say the same sorts of things.[7] And there is surely much to be said for this general position. It is (or should be) clear that there is no simple, unique, ideally adequate concept-framework for "describing the world." The botanist, horticulturist, landscape gardener, farmer, and painter will operate from diverse cognitive "points of view" to describe one self-same vegetable garden. It is mere mythology to think that the "phenomena of nature" lend themselves to only one correct style of descriptive and explanatory conceptualization. There is surely no "ideal scientific language" that has a privileged status for the characterization of reality. As we have noted even in the case of mathematics, different sorts of creatures are bound to make use of different conceptual schemes for the representation of their experience. To insist on the ultimate uniqueness of science is to succumb to "the myth of the God's-eye view." Different cognitive perspectives are possible, no one of them more adequate or more correct than any other independently of the aims and purposes of their users.

As long as the fundamental categories for the characterization of experience—the modes of spatiality and temporality, of structural description, functional connection, and explanatory rationalization—are not seen as necessary features of intelligence as such, but as evolved cognitive adaptations to particular contingently constituted modes of emplacement in and interaction with nature, there will be no reason to expect uniformity. Sociologists of knowledge tell us that even for us humans here on earth, our Western science is but one of many competing ways of conceptualizing the world's processes. And when one turns outward toward space at large, the prospects of diversity become virtually endless.

The idea of conceptually different science is usefully illuminated by casting the issue in temporal rather than spatial terms. The descriptive characterization of *alien* science is a project rather akin in its difficulty to that of describing our own *future* science. It is a key fact of life that progress in science is a process of *ideational* innovation that always places certain developments outside the intellectual horizons of earlier workers. The very concepts we think in terms of become available only in the course of scientific discovery itself. Like the science of the remote future, the science of remote aliens must be presumed to be such that we really could not achieve intellectual access to it on the basis of our own achieved position in the cognitive scheme of things. Just as the technology of a more advanced civilization would be bound to strike us as magic, so its science would be bound to strike us as incomprehensible gibberish—until we had learned it "from the ground up." They might (just barely) be able to *teach* it to us, but they could not *explain* it to us by transposing it into our terms. Differing radically in mode of formulation, in subject-matter orientation, and in conceptualization, their science could well be something that we could not begin to recognize as such.

(4) The One-World, One-Science Argument

One writer on extraterrestrial intelligence poses the question: "What can we talk about with our remote friends?" and answers with the remark: "We have a lot in common. We have mathematics in common, and physics, and astronomy."[8] Another maintains that "we may fail to enjoy their music, understand their poetry, or approve their ideals, but we can talk about matters of practical and scientific concern."[9] But is it all that simple? With respect to his hypothetical Planetarians, the ingenious Christiaan Huygens wrote, three centuries ago:

> Well, but allowing these Planetarians some sort of reason, must it needs be the same with ours? Why truly I think 'tis, and must be so; whether we consider it as applied to Justice and Morality, or exercised in the Principles and Foundations of Science. . . . For the aim and design of the Creator is everywhere the preservation and safety of his Creatures. Now when such a reason as we are masters of, is necessary for the preservation of Life, and promoting of Society (a thing that they be not without, as we shall show) would it not be strange that the Planetarians should have such a perverse sort of Reason given them, as would necessarily destroy and confound what it was design'd to maintain and defend? But allowing Morality and Passions with those Gentlemen to be somewhat different from ours, . . . yet still there would be no doubt, but that in the search after Truth, in judging of the consequences of things, in reasoning, particularly in that form which belongs to Magnitude or Quantity about which their Geometry (if they have such a thing) is employ'd, there would be no doubt I say, but that their Reason here must be exactly the same, and go the same way to work with ours, and that what's true in one part will hold true over the whole Universe; so that all the difference must lie in the degree of Knowledge, which will be proportional to the Genius and Capacity of the Inhabitants.[10]

It is doubtless tempting to reason: "Since there is only one nature, only one science of nature is possible." Yet, on closer scrutiny, this reasoning becomes highly problematic. Above all, it fails to reckon with the fact that while there indeed is only one world, nevertheless very different *thought-worlds* can be at issue in the elaboration of a "science."

It is surely naive to think that because one single object is in question, its description must issue in one uniform result. This view ignores the crucial impact of the describer's intellectual orientation. Minds with different concerns and interests and with different experiential backgrounds can deal with the selfsame items in ways that yield wholly disjointed and disparate results because different features of the thing are being addressed. The *things* are the same, but their significance is altogether different.

Perhaps it seems plausible to argue thus: "Common problems constrain common solutions. Intelligent alien civilizations have in. common with us the problem of cognitive accommodation to a shared world. Natural science as we know it is *our* solution to this problem. Therefore, it is likely to be *theirs* as well." But this tempting argument founders on its second premise. The problem-situation confronted by extraterrestrials is *not* common with ours. Their situation must be presumed substantially different exactly because they live in a significantly different environment and come equipped with significantly different resources—physical and intellectual alike. The common problems, common solutions line does not work: to presuppose a common problem is already to beg the question.

Science is always the result of *inquiry* into nature, and this is inevitably a matter of a *transaction* or *interaction* in which nature is but one party and the inquiry being another. We must expect alien beings to question nature in ways very different from our own. On the basis of an *interactionist* model, there is no reason to think that the sciences of different civilizations will exhibit anything more than the roughest sorts of family resemblance.

Our alien scientific colleagues also scan nature for regularities, perforce using (at any rate, to begin with) the sensors provided to them by their evolutionary heritage. They note, record, and transmit those regularities that they find to be useful or interesting, and then develop their inquiries by theoretical triangulation from this basis. Now, this is clearly going to make for a course of development that closely gears their science to their particular situation—their biological endowment ("their sensors"), their cultural heritage ("what is pragmatically useful"). Where these key parameters differ, we must expect that the course of scientific development will differ as well.

Admittedly, there is only one universe, and its laws and materials are, as far as we can tell, the same everywhere. We share this common universe with all life-forms. However radically we differ in other respects (in particular, those relating to environment, to natural endowments, and to style or civilization), we have a common background of cosmic evolution and a common heritage of natural laws. And so, if intelligent aliens investigate nature at all, they will investigate the same nature we ourselves do. All this can be agreed. But the fact remains that the corpus of scientific information—ours or anyone's—is an ideational construction. And the sameness of the object of contemplation does nothing to guarantee the sameness of ideas about it. It is all too familiar a fact that even where only human observers are at issue, very different constructions are often placed upon "the same" occurrences. As is clearly shown by the rival interpretations of different psychological schools—to say nothing of the court testimony of rival "experts"—there need be little uniformity in the conceptions held about one self-same object from different "perspectives of consideration." The fact that all intelligent beings inhabit the same world does not countervail the no less momentous fact that we inhabit very different ecological niches within it, engendering very different sorts of *modus operandi.*

There is no categorical assurance that intelligent creatures will think alike in a common world, any more than they will act alike—that is, there is no reason why *cognitive* adaptation should be any more uniform than *behavioral* adaptation. Thought, after all, is simply a kind of action; and as the action of a creature reflects its biological heritage, so too does its mode of thought.

The development of a "science"—a specific codification of the laws of nature—always requires as input some inquirer-supplied element of determination. The result of such an interaction depends crucially on the contribution from both sides—from nature and from the intelligences that interact with it. A kind of "chemistry" is at work in which nature provides only one input and the inquirers themselves provide another—one that can massively and dramatically affect the outcome in such a way that we cannot disentangle the respective contributions of nature and the inquirer. Things cannot of themselves dictate the significance that an active intelligence can attach to them. Human organisms are essentially similar, but there is not much similarity between the medicine of the ancient Hindus and that of the ancient Greeks.

No one who has observed how very differently the declarations of a single text (the *Bible,* say, or the dialogues of Plato) have been interpreted and understood over the centuries— even by people of a common cultural heritage—can be unalloyedly hopeful that the study of a common object by different civilizations must lead to a uniform result. Even this textual analogy is overly generous. The scientific study of nature is not a matter of decoding a pre-existing text. There just is no one fixed basic text—the changeless "book of nature writ large"—that different civilizations can decipher in different degrees. Like other books, it is to some extent a mirror: what looks out depends on who looks in.

After all, throughout the earlier stages of man's intellectual history, different human civilizations developed their "natural sciences" in substantially different ways. The shift to an extraterrestrial setting is bound to amplify this diversity. The "science" of an alien civilization may be far more remote from ours than the "language" of our cousin the dolphin is remote from our language. We must face, however reluctantly, the fact that on a cosmic scale the "hard" physical sciences have something of the same cultural relativity that one encounters with the "softer" social sciences on a terrestrial basis.

The theses and theories of our science are necessarily based on "the available data" and accordingly reflect the character of our interactions with nature—through which alone data can be acquired. This interaction is a two-sided process to which each party makes an essential contribution—and where the character of these respective contributions cannot be altogether distinguished and clearly separated. Here, the potential plurality of modes of judgment means that there is no single definitive way of knowing the world.

Charles Sanders Peirce held that truth is "the predestined result to which sufficient enquiry would ultimately lead,"[11] since "let any human being have enough information and exert enough thought upon any question, and the result will be that he will arrive at a certain definite conclusion, which is the same as that which any other mind will reach under sufficiently favorable circumstances."[12] For Peirce, if there is any prospect of truth at all, if any "fact of the matter" exists, then all inquirers are ultimately destined to achieve agreement about it. But even if one grants this (surely problematic) thesis of an ultimate uniformity of result in *human* inquiry, there is no good reason to project this uniformity across species—to see product as independent of process in that different inquiry species must ultimately arrive at the same results. Our "scientific truths" are not necessarily those of others.

Natural science—broadly construed as inquiry into the ways of nature—is something that is, in principle, endlessly plastic. Its development will trace out an historical course closely geared to the specific capacities, interest, environment, and opportunities of the creatures that develop it. We are deeply mistaken if we think of it as a process that must follow a route generally parallel to ours and issue in a roughly comparable product. It would be grossly unimaginative to think that either the journey or the destination must be the same—or even substantially similar.

The science of the species like the behavior of the individual is captive to a biological and cultural heritage. Factors such as capacities, requirements, interests, and course of development are bound to affect the shape and substance of the science and technology of any particular space-time region. Unless we narrow our intellectual horizons in a parochially anthropomorphic way, we must be prepared to recognize the great likelihood that the "science" and "technology" of a remote civilization would be something *very* different from science and technology as we know it. Our human sort of natural science may well be unique in its kind, adjusted to and coordinated with a being of our physical constitution, inserted into the orbit of the world's processes and history in our sort of way.

These considerations point to a clear lesson. Different civilizations composed of different sorts of creatures must be expected to create diverse "sciences." Each inquiring civilization must be expected to produce its own, perhaps ever-changing, cognitive products—all more or less adequate in their own ways, but with little if any actual overlap in conceptual content. Though inhabiting the same physical universe with us, and subject to the same sorts of fundamental regularities, they must be expected to produce as cognitive

artifacts different depictions of nature, reflecting their different modes of emplacement within it. The one-world, one-
science argument is ultimately untenable.

(5) Evolutionary Ramifications

The ultimate reason why we cannot expect alien intelligences to be engaged in doing our sort of science is that the
possible sorts of "natural science" are almost endlessly diverse.
Sciences—understood as such in the functional-equivalency
terms laid down above—are bound to vary with the cognitive
instruments available in the physical constitution and mental
equipment of their developers and with the cognitive focus of
interest of their cultural perspective and conceptual framework. Our cognitive project is simply the intellectual product
characteristic of one particular sort of cognitive life-form.
There is accordingly good reason to see natural science as
species-relative.

With respect to biological evolution it seems perfectly
sensible to reason as follows: "What can we say about the
forms of life evolving on these other worlds? . . . [It] is clear
that subsequent evolution by natural selection would lead to
an immense variety of organisms; compared to them, all
organisms on Earth, from molds to men, are very close
relations."[13] Exactly the same situation will surely obtain with
respect to cognitive evolution.

And what assurance is there that even intelligent beings
will engender a "science"? The developmental path from
intelligence to science is, after all, strewn with substantial
obstacles. Matters must be propitious not just as regards the
physics, chemistry, biochemistry, evolutionary biology, and
cognitive psychology of the situation; the sociological requis-
ites for the evolution of science as a cultural artifact must also
be met. Economic conditions, social organization, and cul-

tural orientation must all be properly adjusted before the move from intelligence to science can be accomplished. For scientific inquiry to evolve and flourish, there must, in the first place, be cultural institutions whose development requires specific economic conditions and a favorable social organization. And terrestrial experience suggests that such conditions for the social evolution of a developed culture are by no means always present where intelligence is. (We would do well to recall that of the hundreds of human civilizations evolved here on earth, only one—the Mediterranean/European—managed to inaugurate natural science as we understand it.)

One recent writer declares: "Since man's existence on the earth occupies but an instant in cosmic time, surely intelligent life has progressed far beyond our level on some of these 100,000,000 (habitable) planets [in our galaxy]."[14] Such reasoning overlooks the critical probabilistic dimension. Admittedly, cosmic locales are very numerous. But when probabilities get to be very small, they will offset this fact. (No matter how massive N is, there is always that diminutive $1/N$ able to countervail it.) Even though there are an immense number of solar systems, and thus a staggering number of sizable planets (some 10^{22} by current estimates), nevertheless, a very substantial number of conditions must be met for "science" (as we understand it) to arise. The astrophysical, physical, chemical, biological, psychological, sociological, and epistemological parameters must all be in proper adjustment. There must be habitability, and life, and intelligence, and culture, and technology, and a technologically geared mode of inquiry and an appropriate subject-matter orientation of this intellectual product, and so on. The successful transition from intelligence to science is nowise a certainty. A great many turnings must go all right *en route* for "science" of a mode comparable to ours to develop. Each step along the way is one of finite (and often small) probability. To reach the final destination, all these probabilities must be multiplied together, yielding a quantity that will be very small indeed. Even if there were only twelve turning points along this developmental route, each involving a chance of successful eventuation that is, on average, no worse than one in one hundred, the chance of an overall success would be diminutively small, corresponding to an aggregate success-probability of merely 10^{-24}. By this reckoning, the number of civilizations that possess a technologized science as we comprehend it is clearly not going to be very substantial: it might, in fact, be strikingly close to 1.

George G. Simpson has rightly stressed the many chance twists and turns that lie along the evolutionary road, insisting that

> the fossil record shows very clearly that there is no central line leading steadily, in a goal-directed way, from a protozoan to man. Instead there has been continual and extremely intricate branching, and whatever course we follow through the branches there are repeated changes both in the rate and in the direction of evolution. Man is the end of one ultimate twig. . . . Even slight changes in earlier parts of the history would have profound cumulative effects on all descendent organisms through the succeeding millions of generations. . . . The existing species would surely have been different if the start had been different, and if any stage of the histories of organisms and their environments had been different. Thus the existence of our present species depends on a very precise sequence of causative events through some two billion years or more. Man cannot be an exception to this rule. If the causal chain had been different, *homo sapiens* would not exist.[15]

The workings of evolution—be it of life or intelligence or culture or technology or science—are always the product of a great number of individually unlikely events. Any evolutionary process involves putting to nature a sequence of questions whose successive resolution produces a series reminiscent of the game "20 Questions," sweeping over a possibility-spectrum of awesomely large proportions. The result eventually reached lies along a route that traces out one particular contingent path within a possibility-space that encompasses an ever-divergent fanning out of alternatives as each step opens up yet further eventuations. An evolutionary process is a very iffy proposition—a complex labyrinth in which a great many twists and turns in the road must be taken aright for matters to end up as they do.

If things had not turned out suitably at each stage, we would not be here to tell the tale. The many contingencies on the long route of cosmic, galactic, solar-system, biochemical, biological, social, cultural, and cognitive evolution have all turned out right; the innumerable obstacles have all been surmounted. In retrospect, it all looks easy and inevitable. The innumerable (unrealized) possibilities of variation along the way are easily kept out of sight and out of mind. The Whig interpretation of history beckons comfortably. It is so easy, so tempting, to say that a planet on which there is life will, of course, evolve a species with the technical capacity for interstellar communications.[16] It is tempting, but it is also nonsense. There are simply too many critical turnings along the road of cosmic and biological evolution. The fact is that many junctures along the way are such that, had things gone only a little differently, we would not be here at all.[17]

The ancient Greek atomists' theory of possibility affords an interesting lesson in this connection. Adopting a Euclideanly infinitistic view of space, they held to a theory of innumerable worlds:

> There are innumerable worlds, which differ in size. In some worlds there is no sun and moon, in others they are larger than in our world, and others more numerous. The intervals between the worlds are unequal; in some parts there are more worlds, in others fewer; some are increasing, some at their height, some decreasing; in some parts they are arising, in

others failing. They are destroyed by collision one with another. There are some worlds devoid of living creatures or
plants or any moisture.[18]

On this basis, the atomists taught that every (suitably
general) possibility is realized in fact someplace or other.
Confronting the question of "Why do dogs not have horns;
just why is the theoretical possibility that dogs be horned not
actually realized?" the atomist replied that it indeed is realized, but just elsewhere—*in another region of space.* Somewhere
within infinite space, there is another world just like ours in
every respect save one: that its dogs have horns. That dogs
lack horns is simply a parochial idiosyncrasy of the particular
local world in which we interlocutors happen to find ourselves. Reality accommodates all possibilities of world alternative to this through spatial distribution: as the atomists saw
it, *all* alternative possibilities are, in fact, actualized in the
various subworlds embraced within one spatially infinite su-
perworld.

This theory of virtually open-ended possibilities was shut
off by the closed cosmos of the Aristotelian world-picture,
which dominated European cosmological thought for almost
two milennia. The break-up of the Aristotelian model in the
Renaissance and its replacement by the "Newtonian" model
is one of the great turning points of the intellectual tradition
of the West—elegantly portrayed in Alexandre Koyré's splen-
didly entitled book, *From the Closed World to the Infinite
Universe.*[19] One may recall Giordano Bruno's near-demonic
delight with the explosion of the closed Aristotelian world
into one opening into an infinite universe spread throughout
endless spaces. Others were not delighted but appalled: John
Donne spoke of "all cohearance lost," and Pascal was fright-
ened by "the eternal silence of infinite spaces" of which he
spoke so movingly in the *Pensées.* But no one doubted that
the onset of the "Newtonian" world-picture represented a
cataclysmic event in the development of Western thought.

Strangely enough, the refinitization of the universe effected by Einstein's general relativity produced scarcely a ripple in philosophical or theological circles, despite the immense stir caused by other aspects of the Einsteinian revolution. (Einsteinian space-time is, after all, even more radically finitistic than the Aristotelian world-picture, which left open, at any rate, the prospect of an infinite future with respect to time.)

To be sure, it might perhaps seem that the finitude in question is not terribly significant because the distances and times involved in modern cosmology are so enormous. But this view is rather naive. The difference between the finite and the infinite is as big as differences can get to be. And it represents a difference that is—in this present context—of the most far-reaching significance. For it means that we have no alternative to supposing that a highly improbable set of eventuations is not going to be realized in very many places, and that something sufficiently improbable may well not be realized at all. The decisive *philosophical* importance of cosmic finitude lies in the fact that in a finite universe only a finite range of alternatives can be realized. A finite universe must "make up its mind" about its contents in a far more radical way than an infinite one, and this is particularly manifest in the context of low-probability possibilities. In a finite world, unlike an infinite one, we cannot avoid supposing that a prospect that is sufficiently unlikely is simply not going to be realized at all, that in piling improbability on improbability we eventually outrun the reach of the actual. It is therefore quite conceivable that our science represents a solution to the problem of cognitive accommodation that is terrestrially locale-specific.

And so we are well advised to accept that the science *as we know it* is merely OUR science—the projection on the screen of mind of a world-picture devised in characteristically human terms of reference. The world is real enough, independently of our ideas about it, but the-world-as-we-view-it on the basis of our inquirers—the only world with which we have *cognitive* as opposed to *causal* interactions—is a construction of ours correlative to our (characteristically human) place in the cosmic scheme. Being the product of our *experience* of nature, our empirical science is bound to reflect, at least in part, the peculiar character of our evolutionary heritage.

A Relativistic Realism

Immanuel Kant's insight holds: there is good reason to think that natural science as we know it is not something universally valid for all rational intelligences as such, but a (partially) man-made creation that is, in crucial respects, correlative with our specifically human intelligence. We have little alternative to supposing that our science is limited precisely by its being *our* science. The inevitability of an empiricism that accepts the fundamentality of experience for our scientific knowledge of the world means that this knowledge is bound to be relativised ultimately to the kinds of experiences we can have. Our science is destined to reflect our nature—to be conditioned and delimited by the sorts of creatures we are with respect to our mode of "sensory" involvement in the world's scheme of things. The "scientific truth" that we discover about the world is *our* truth—not so much in the sense that "we make it up" in an arbitrary way, but rather in the sense that, since science is *empirical* science, it is bound to be conditioned by our human mode of emplacement within nature.

There just is no unique itinerary of scientific/technological development that different civilizations travel in common with mere differences in speed or in staying power (notwithstanding the penchant of astrophysicists for the neat plotting of numerical "degrees of development" against time in the evolution of planetary civilizations).[20] In cognitive and even in "scientific" evolution, we are not dealing with a single railway line but with a complex network leading to very different destinations. Even as cosmic evolution involves a spatial red shift that carries different star systems ever farther from each other, so cognitive evolution may well involve an intellectual red shift that carries different civilizations into thought-worlds ever more remote from each other.

This approach supports a scientific realism all right, but only a realism that is relativistic in that its insistence on the multi-faceted nature of the real means that any science will reflect its deviser's particular "slant" on reality (in line with the investigator-characteristic modes of interaction with nature). On such a view, knowledge of reality is always (in some crucial respect) cast in terms of reference that reflect its possessor's cognitive proceedings. There is, no doubt, a mind-independent reality, but cognitive access to it is always mind-conditioned. All that can ever be known of reality is mediated through conceptions that reflect *how this reality affects* us, given to the sensory and cognitive endowments with which our evolutionary heritage has equipped us.

NOTES

1. Obviously, no sensible relativism can maintain that "*everything is relative,*" thereby pulling the mat out from under its own feet. Relativism must be developed with respect to a limited range; one cannot say, "No proposition is to be asserted absolutely" but only, "No proposition belonging to the range R is to be asserted absolutely—where this proposition itself should of course not belong to R. But this is all we need for present purposes, seeing that the thesis, "The contentions of natural science are man-relativized" is of course itself not a contention of natural science. It is a thesis *about* the domain, rather than one lying *within* it.

2. For a useful account of the historical background of this line of speculation, see Frank J. Tigler, "A Brief History of the Extraterrestrial Intelligence Concept" in the *Quarterly Journal of the Royal Astronomical Society,* vol. 22 (1981), pp. 133–145.

3. Compare the discussion in Goesta Ehrensvaerd, *Man on Another World* tr. by L. and K. Roden (Chicago: University of Chicago Press, 1965), pp. 146–148.

4. Georg Simmel, "Ueber eine Beziehung der Selektionslehre zur Erkenntnistheorie," *Archiv für systematische Philosophie und Soziologie*, vol. 1 (1985), pp. 34–35 (see pp. 40–41).

5. William James, *Pragmatism* (New York: Longmans Green, 1907).

6. His anthropological investigations pointed Benjamin Lee Whorf in much this same direction. He wrote: "The real question is: What do different languages do, not with artificially isolated objects, but with the flowing face of nature in its motion, color, and changing form; with clouds, beaches, and yonder flight of birds? For as goes our segmentation of the face of nature, so goes our physics of the cosmos" ("Language and Logic," in *Language, Thought, Reality*, ed. by J. B. Carroll [Cambridge, Mass.: Harvard University Press, 1956], pp. 240–241). Compare also the interesting discussion in Thomas Nagel, "What is it Like to Be a Bat?" in *Mortal Questions* (Cambridge: Cambridge University Press, 1979).

7. Thomas Kuhn, *The Structure of Scientific Revolutions* (Chicago: University of Chicago Press, 1962).

8. See E. Purcell in *Interstellar Communication: A Collection of Reprints and Original Contributions.* ed. by A.G.W. Cameron (New York and Amsterdam, 1963).

9. Paul Anderson, *Is There Life on Other Worlds?* (New York: Crowell-Collier, 1963), p. 130.

10. Christiaan Huygens, *Cosmotheoros: The Celestial Worlds Discovered—New Conjectures Concerning the Planetary Worlds, Their Inhabitants and Productions* 2nd ed. (London: James Knapton, 1698), pp. 41–43.

11. C. S. Peirce, *Collected Papers*, vol. V, sect. 5.494.

12. *Ibid.*, 8.12.

13. I. S. Shklovskii and Carl Sagan, *Intelligent Life in the Universe*, tr. by Paula Fern (San Francisco: Holden Day, 1966), p. 350.

14. See. M. Calvin in A.G.W. Cameron (ed.), *op. cit.* p. 75.

15. George Gaylord Simpson, "The Nonprevalence of Humanoids," *Science*, vol. 143 (1964), pp. 769–775, reprinted as Chapter

13 of *This View of Life: The World of an Evolutionist* (New York: Scribner, 1964), see pp. 773–4.

16. See A.G.W. Cameron (ed.), *op. cit.*

17. Robert T. Rood and James S. Trefil, *Are We Alone? The Possibility of Extraterrestrial Civilization* (New York: Scribner, 1981).

18. Diels-Kranz 68 A 40 [for Leucippus and Democritus]; tr. G. S. Kirk and J. E. Raven, *The Presocratic Philosophers* (Cambridge, 1957), p. 411.

19. Alexandre Koyré, *From the Closed World to the Infinite Universe* (New York: Harper, 1957).

20. John A. Ball, "Extraterrestrial Intelligence: Where is Everybody?". *American Scientist*, vol. 68 (1980), pp. 565–663 (see p. 658).

SIX

Evolution as an Allocation Mechanism

SYNOPSIS

(1) We humans are smart because we have to fit into our evolutionary niche. Intelligence is the characteristic specialty that constitutes the comparative advantage by which our species has made its evolutionary way down the corridor of time. (2) We humans are so dumb because it would actually be evolutionarily counterproductive for us to be substantially smarter than we are.

---

(1) Why Are We So Smart?

Why are we humans so smart? How is it that we possess the intellectual talent to create mathematics, medicine, science, engineering, architecture, literature, and other comparably splendid cognitive disciplines? What explains the immense power of our intellectual capacities?

An immediate difficulty looms when this question is posed. "How," an objector urges, "can you possibly set out to explain why we are as intelligent as we are without first addressing the question of just exactly how intelligent we indeed are?" Clearly, if *this* issue had to be settled at the outset, the inquiry would never get off the ground. The available time and effort would be consumed in preliminary clarifications. But, in fact, this matter of extent only concerns us in a *comparative* way here. The pertinent analogy is that of considering why we humans are so relatively tall on the basis of our being taller than our distant cousins, the chimpanzees. And the cardinal point would be that nonamphibious humanoids could not be chimpanzee-size without undue loss of brain capacity. (And by a comparable token, we couldn't be taller than giraffes and still free that second pair of limbs from transport service.) Similarly, what concerns us here is simply the rough, comparative issue of our capacity as intelligent agents to outdistance the other terrestrial species by a very substantial margin in regard to intelligence-guided capabilities.

The *general* direction—at any rate—of the answer to this query about human intelligence is relatively straightforward. Basically, we are so smart because that is our place in evolution's scheme of things. Different sorts of creatures have different ecological niches, different specialties that enable them to find their evolutionary way down the corridor of time. Some are highly prolific, some very hard, some swift of foot, some hard to spot, some extremely shy. *Homo sapiens* is different. For the evolutionary instrument of our species is *intelligence* with everything that this involves in the way of abilities and versatilities. Thus, if we weren't so intelligent, we wouldn't be here as the creatures we are. We have all those splendid intellectual capacities because we require them in order to be ourselves.

Of course it's not all just a matter of luck—of fate's lottery bringing intelligence our way. Evolution's bio-engineering is the crucial factor. Bees and termites can achieve impressive prodigies of collective effort. But an insect developed under the aegis of evolution could not become as smart as a man because information-processing needs of the lifestyle opportunities afforded by its physical endowment are too modest to push it to the development of intelligence.

Smarts are an inherent concomitant of our physical endowment. Our bodies have many more independently movable parts (more "degrees of freedom") than those of most other creatures.[1] And this circumstance has significant implications. For suppose a system with n switches, each capable of assuming an ON or OFF position. Then there are 2^n states in which the system can find itself. With $n = 3$ there are only 8 system-states, but with n doubling to 6 there are already 64 states. As a body grows more complex and its configuration takes on more degrees of freedom, the range of alternative possible states expands rapidly (exponentially). Merely keeping track of its actual position is already difficult. To plan ahead is more difficult yet. If there are m possible states which the system can assume now, then when it comes to selecting its next position there are also m choices, and for the next two there are $m \times m$ alternatives overall (ignoring unrealizable combinations). So with a two-step planning horizon the 3-state system has 64 alternatives while that 6-state system has 4096. With a mere doubling of states, the planning problem has become complicated by a factor of sixty-four.

The degrees of freedom inherent in variable movement over time are pivotal considerations here. The moment one walks upright and begins to develop the modes of motion that this new posture facilitates—by way of creeping, running, leaping, etc.—one has many more problems of physical management to solve.

Considerations of this sort render it evident that a vertebrate having a more highly articulated skeleton, with many independently operable bones and bone-complexes, faces vastly greater difficulties in management and manipulation—in what military jargon calls "command and control." Physically more versatile animals have to be smarter simply because they are physically more versatile.

We are driven to ever greater capabilities in information acquisition and management by the greater demands of the lifestyle of our ecological niche. The complexity of our sophisticated surveillance mechanisms in the context of friend-or-foe identification is an illustration. We can observe at a considerable distance that people are looking at us, discriminating minute differences in eye orientation in this context. The development of our sophisticated senses with their refined discrimination of odors, colors, and sounds is another example. Environmental surveillance is crucial for our lifestyle. We have to know which features of our environment to heed and which can safely be ignored. The handling of such a volume of information calls for selectivity and for sophisticated processing mechanisms—for intelligence, in short. Not only must our bodies be the right size to support our physical operations and activities, but our brains must be so as well.

The complexities of information management and control pose unrelenting evolutionary demands. To process a large volume of information, nature must fit us out with a large brain. A battleship needs more elaborate mechanisms for guidance and governance than a row boat. A department store needs a more elaborate managerial apparatus than a corner grocery. To operate a sophisticated body you need a sophisticated brain. The evolution of the human brain is the story of nature's struggles to provide the machinery of information management and control needed by creatures of increasing physical versatility. A feedback cycle comes into operation—a complex body requires a larger brain for command and control, and a larger brain requires a larger body whose operational efficiency in turn places greater demands on that brain for the managerial functions required to provide for survival and the assurance of a posterity. As can be illustrated by comparing the brain weights of different mammalian species, the growing complexities and versatilities of animal bodies involve a physical lifestyle whose difficulties of information processing and management requires an increasingly powerful brain. How one makes one's living also matters: insect-eating and fruit-eating monkeys have heavier brains, for their size, than leaf-eating one's do.[2]

Here then is the immediate (and rather trivial) answer to

our question: We are as intelligent as we are because that is how we had to evolve to fill our place in nature's scheme of things. We are so smart because evolution's bio-engineering needs to provide those smarts for us to achieve and maintain the lifestyle appropriate to our ecological niche.

But there remains the problem of why evolution would take this course? Surely we didn't need to be *that* smart to outwit the saber toothed tiger or domesticate the sheep. Let us explore this aspect of the matter a little.

The things we have to do to manage our lifestyle must not only be *possible* for us, they must in general be *easy* for us (so easy that most of them can be done unthinkingly and even unconsciously). If our problem-solving resources were frequently strained to the limit, often groaning under the weight of difficulty of the problems they are called on by nature to solve in the interests of our lifestyle, then we just wouldn't have it.

For evolution to do its work, the survival problems that creatures confront have to be, by and large, easy for the mechanisms at their disposal. And this fundamental principle holds just as true for cognitive as for biological evolution. If cognitive problem-solving were too difficult for our mental resources, we wouldn't evolve as problem solving creatures. If we had to go to as great lengths to work our 2 + 2 as to extract the cube root of a number, or if it took us as long to discriminate 3- from 4-sided figures as it takes to discriminate between 296- and 297-sided ones, then these sorts of issues would simply remain outside our cognitive repertoire. The "average" problems for survival and thriving that are posed by our lifestyle must be of the right level of difficulty for us—that is, they must be relatively easy. And that calls for excess capacity. All of the "ordinary" problems of one's mode of life must be solvable quickly in real time—and with enough idle capacity left over to cope with the unusual.

A brain that is able to do the necessary things when and as

needed to sustain the life of a complex and versatile creature will remain underutilized most of the time. To cope at times of peak demand, it will have a great deal of excess capacity to spare for other issues at slack times. And so, any brain powerful enough to accomplish those occasionally necessary tasks will have the excess capacity at most normal times to pursue various challenging projects that have nothing whatever to do with survival.

These deliberations resolve the objection that evolution cannot explain our intelligence because we are a lot smarter than evolution demands—that, after all, evolution does not set us examinations on higher mathematics or theoretical physics. What is being maintained here is not the absurd contention that such disciplines somehow afford humans with an evolutionary advantage. All that is being said is that the capacities and abilities that make a realization of these enterprises possible are evolutionarily advantageous. That evolution equips us with a reserve capacity that makes these activities possible is a side benefit. The point is that an intelligent creature whose capacities do not allow for development in these directions just isn't smart enough to pass evolution's examinations in other matters—that is, wouldn't be able to make intelligence its evolutionary specialty after all.

The brain/computer analogy once again proves helpful in this connection. Very different things can be at stake with being "simple": the simplicity of "hardware" at issue with comparatively less complex *computers* is one sort of thing, and the simplicity of "software" at issue with comparatively less complex *programs* is something quite different. And there are clearly trade-offs here. Solving problems of the same level of difficulty is generally easier to program on more sophisticated (more complex) computing machines. Something of an inverse relationship obtains: greater machine complication can make the actual use of the machine easier and less demanding. It is generally less difficult to program more "advanced" (i.e., complex) machines to do various sorts of tasks. And this circumstance is reflected in the fact that a creature which makes its evolutionary way in the world by intelligence requires a rather powerful and complicated brain.

To be sure, evolution is not, in general, over-generous. For example, evolution will not develop creatures whose running-speed is vastly greater than what is needed to escape their predators, to catch their prey, or to realize some other such strictly utilitarian objective. But intelligence and its works are a clear exception to this general rule, owing to its self-catalyzing nature. With *cognitive* artifacts as with many *physical* artifacts, the character of the issues prevents a holding back. And once one can do a little with calculation or with information processing, one can, in principle, do a lot. Once evolution lets intelligence in through the door, it gets "the run of the house." When bio-design takes the route of intelligence to secure an evolutionary advantage for a creature, it embarks on a slippery slope. Having started along this road, there is no easy and early stop. For once a species embarks on intelligence as its instrument for coping with nature, then the pressure of species-internal competition enters as a hot-house forcing process. Intelligence itself becomes a goad to further development simply because intelligence is, as it were, developmentally self-energizing.

The result of the preceding deliberations is straight forward. Intelligence is the evolutionary specialty *of homo sapiens*. If we were markedly less smart than we in fact are, we would not have been able to survive. Or rather, more accurately, we would not have been able to develop into the sort of creatures we have become. Intelligence constitutes the characteristic specialty that provides the comparative advantage that has enabled our species to make its evolutionary way into this world's scheme of things. We are so smart because this is necessary for *us* to be here at all.

(2) Why Are We So Dumb?

But at this point a very different question arises, one that points in the exactly opposite direction: Why aren't we a great deal more intelligent than we, in fact, are? Why can't we master a foreign language within a single week's effort or learn calculus in a fortnight? What explains our manifest cognitive deficits and limitations? Why are we so dumb?

This question is also one that can, in principle, be answered in evolutionary terms.[3] But it has two importantly different aspects: (i) Why aren't we *comprehensively* smarter by way of enhanced mind-power for the species as a whole; and (ii) Why aren't we *statistically* smarter by way of an increase in the relative proportion of smart people within the presently constituted range of intelligence levels. Let us consider these issues one at a time.

To be a substantially smarter species, we would, for starters, need a much bigger brain. To manage this on prevailing bioengineering principles would require a larger, less agile body, forcing us to forego the advantages of maneuverability and versatility. To process twice the information would require a brain of roughly four times its present size. But to quadruple our brain-weight we would need a body of sixteen times it present weight.[4] A body of so great a weight is not only extremely cumbersome but involves enormous demands for energy. The most plausible and probable move would then be to opt for a very different ecological niche and take to the water, joining our mammalian cousins the whales and dolphins. The stimulating surroundings of a land environment with its invitations to communal socialization, division of labor, and technological development would all be denied us. That gain in brain power would have come at an awesome cost, the sacrifice of the collective intelligence of the social institutionalization of tool-using creatures. The price is one that evolution cannot afford.[5]

There remains, however, the question of why we humans should not be smarter by way of a statistical improvement in the *proportion* of very smart people in our existing species? With this shift of questions, we now move from the issue of bio-engineering a "more intelligent" *species* to the development of a "more intelligent" *population*—one in which the percentage of people who would qualify as "superior" in intelligence by *present* standards would be substantially enlarged.

Here the social dimension of the matter comes into prominence. Consider the following sort of case. You and I interact in a competitive situation of potential benefit that has roughly zero-sum character, with one party's gain as the other's loss. Two alternatives are open to each of us: to COLLABORATE with the other, or to try to OUTWIT him. If we collaborate, we shall share the resultant benefit (say by each getting one-half it). If we compete, then the winner takes all; whoever succeeds gains the whole benefit. The overall situation thus stands as depicted in Display 1. If I see my chances of winning as given by the probability p, then my expectations stand as follows:

$$EV \text{ (collaborate)} = p\,(0.5\ B) + (1 - p)\,(0.5\ B) = 0.5\ B$$

$$EV \text{ (compete)} = p\,(B) + (1 - p)\,(0) = p\,(B)$$

Display 1

HYPOTHETICAL PAYOFFS
IN A SITUATION OF COMPETITION

	Fortune favors me	*Fortune favors you*
We collaborate	0.5 B/0.5 B	0.5 B/0.5 B
We fail to collaborate	B/0	0/B

Note: The table entry x/y represents the gains for the two parties x for me and y for you, respectively.

So long as p is less than one-half, that is, as long as my subjectively appraised chances of winning are less than even, collaboration is the sensible course relative to the balance of expectations. But when p exceeds one-half, the balance moves in favor of noncooperation. If one views the benefits of self-reliance optimistically, then decision-theoretic rationality inclines against cooperation; it favors going one's own competitive way and "taking one's chances." People who see themselves as comparatively more clever are less likely to collaborate.

To picture the structure of the situation more graphically, consider the state of affairs reflected in the (purely hypothetical) statistical distributions pictured in Display 2. If we suppose people interact randomly, then in Case I, well over half (namely 54 percent) of pairwise interpersonal interactions are between cognitive compeers (equals), but in Case II well under one-half (namely 46 percent) of the interactions are so. Given that it takes two to cooperate, the upshot is that in Case I, the majoritarian social norm would be such as to provide a rational impetus to cooperation, but in case II it would militate for noncooperation by trying to outwit.

Display 2

HYPOTHETICAL DISTRIBUTIONS OF COGNITIVE ABILITY

	Highly Able	Moderately Able	Substandardly Able
I. The actual distribution of cognitive ability (hypothetical)	10%	70%	20%
II. A situation of contemplated improvement	30%	60%	10%

Note: the ability levels at issue are to be taken as fixed by the presently prevailing standards.

This artificial quantitative example thus serves a purely qualitative didactic function. Its point is simply that two counterbalancing forces are operative, the one a natural selective impetus that tends toward increasing the proportion of the highly able, and the other, a primarily social tendency, toward the maintenance of a cooperation-compelling diversity. If more humans were comparatively smarter, we would, no doubt, be able to manage various interactions with nature more successfully. Our ability to manipulate our environment cognitively and physically—to explain, predict, control— would be enhanced. But our interactions with one another would be subject to an increased temptation for people confident of their abilities to try to "outsmart" their fellows. Rational calculation regarding potentially competitive interactions would now favor the course of competition, of trying to outwit. The socially beneficial impetus to cooperation provided by a healthy diffidence would become undermined. In a way, statistical inferiority serves as an equalizer. And this is all to the general good. The natural outrage we feel, even as children, against noncooperation and people who do not play fair is patently connected in the evolutionary order with the fact that most of us draw substantial benefits from a system in which people "play by the rules."

Accordingly, if we humans were statistically more intelligent than we are, the greater success of our interactions with nature would incline us towards a yet higher estimation of our intellectual powers, and in consequence the impetus to collaboration with others would become undermined. A statistical enhancement of cognitive competence would tend to increase the number of people who, trusting to their intelligence, would try to outwit others rather than "playing by the rules"— which, after all, are largely designed to protect the non-advantaged. The darkness of general incomprehension creates a smoky battlefield where parties of different levels of ability can contend on a much more even footing. The social cooperation conducive to human well-being overall benefits from general incapacity.

As the bee illustrates, the evolution of cooperation certainly does not require individual intelligence. Quite to the contrary. As the numbers of "clever people" who pride themselves on strength of intellect increases, social cohesion becomes more difficult to obtain. University faculties are notoriously difficult to manage. "Experts" are the thorns in the sides of popes and presidents alike: no sect manages to keep on easy terms with its theologians. (Anyone who is familiar with the ways of an intellectual *avant garde* such as the Bloomsbury circle has some idea of the difficulties of socializing people who see themselves as more than ordinarily clever.) It is easy to envision how in numerous circumstances intelligence militates against cooperation.

We humans require intelligence to structure our interactions with nature into generally beneficial channels. But no less importantly, we are collectively so situated that we need to cooperate and collaborate with one another in ways that conduce to the general benefit. And if we were, on statistical balance, more intelligent than we are, such cooperation and collaboration would be more difficult to achieve. People would become more reliant on their own wits and retreat from reliance on others, deeming themselves as "above the common herd."

An admixture of dumbness is thus evolutionarily advantageous. For an individual's prospects of surviving and thriving are often bound up with how well or ill things are going in the society of which this individual is part (as wars, experiences, and economic depressions indicate). And insofar as a society's well-being can be undermined by a surfeit of intelligent individuals, evolution will (obliquely) select against individual intelligence.

The interesting and perhaps surprising lesson thus emerges that if we humans were, on balance, to be substantially more intelligent than we actually are, then the rational impetus to socialization and cooperation would be undermined. If people were *bodily* stronger than they are, they would have to be larger and heavier—and would thus be hampered physically by the resultant cumbersomeness. If people were *mentally* stronger than they are, they would be hampered socially by a resultant impetus towards trying to outwit one another. The prospect of effective socialization in the service of communal interests and the general good would be reduced. And any such result would clearly be evolutionarily counterproductive. One very good reason why we're not a lot smarter is just that it wouldn't be a very smart move to be so.

(3) Conclusion

These deliberations yield the odd-sounding lesson that evolutionary pressure is a two-edged sword that can act in opposed directions as regards the development of intelligence. Evolution is a process in which the balance of cost and benefit is constantly maintained in a delicate equilibrium. And this general phenomenon is vividly illustrated in the particular case of our cognitive capacities. On the one hand, we humans are not less intelligent than we are because if we were, we would incur an evolutionary disadvantage in our *physical* dealings with nature. But analogously, we are not more intelligent than we are, because if we were, we would *also* suffer an evolutionary disability by becoming disadvantaged in our *social* dealings with one another, since we would no longer feel constrained to cooperate because the course of events drives home the recognition that we're just not smart enough to go it alone. In its handling of intelligence, evolution, like a shrewd gambler, is clever enough to follow the precept: "Quit while you're ahead."

NOTES

1. The human skeleton has some 220 bones, about the same number as a cat when tail bones are excluded. A small monkey has

around 120. Of course, what matters for present purposes is *independently* moving parts. This demotes "thousand leggers" and—thanks to fingers, among other things—takes us out of the cat's league.

2. At any given time in evolutionary history, the then-current herbivores tended to have smaller brains than the contemporary carnivores. See Richard Dawkin, *The Blind Watchmaker* (New York: Norton, 1986), p. 190.

3. It may be thought that there is something incongruous in asking for an evolutionary explanation for something that has not happened. But the issue is rather one of using basic principles of natural process to explain why evolution does not take certain routes. In this regard, the situation with respect to intelligence (i.e., *cognitive* agility) is not dissimiliar from that with regard to motion (i.e., *physical* agility). Explaining why evolution has not produced a hyperintelligent mammal is structurally akin to explaining why it has not produced a hyperswift one by outfitting creatures with organic wheels. For an interesting treatment of this issue see Jared Diamond, "The Biology of the Wheel," *Nature,* vol. 302 (14 April 1983), pp. 572–73.

4. On this issue, compare J.B.S. Haldane's insightful and provocative essay "On Being the Right Size" in his collection *Possible Worlds and Other Papers* (New York: Haynes & Bros., 1928).

5. Of course here—as elsewhere—we cannot let matters rest with speaking of an evolutionary process in this rather anthropomorphic way. In the final analysis, we have to cash in these metaphors in terms of different groups (tribes, clans) of humanoids chancing to produce a bumper crop of more than ordinarily intelligent individuals and finding themselves at a reproductive disadvantage thereby because of their comparatively greater risk-aversiveness. But no imaginative student of recent demographic phenomena will find difficulty in envisioning an appropriate sort of scenario here.

SEVEN

Does A Darwinian Account of the Origin of Mind Preclude Intentionality and Purpose?

SYNOPSIS

(1) It is sometimes said that a Darwinian evolutionary account of the origins of mind leaves no room for meaning and purpose in the domain of human doings and dealings. (2) Such an objection fails to heed the necessary distinction between the issues of *causal origination* and *hermeneutical explanation* of human phenomena. Natural selection can and does account causally for how being with certain capacities can arise and how they operate in the exercise of these capacities; but it does not and cannot provide an account of what exercising these capacities is like from an experiential perspective. And intentionally (purposiveness, meaning, valuation, and the like) is part of this internalized, experiential perspective, and cannot be properly comprehended from an external, causal point of departure. (3) But incompleteness is one thing and defectiveness quite another. Different questions are at issue. Evolutionary epistemology cannot fairly be faulted on a charge of incapacity because it does not treat matters that lie outside its sphere—issues it makes no pretense to address at all. Nor, of course, can it *conflict* with such matters, let alone *exclude* them.

(1) Does Evolution Eradicate Purpose?

Philosophers and scientists sometimes maintain that a Darwinian evolutionary account of the origin of mind and its operations is bound to be deficient because it leaves no room for intentionality, with the result that *meaning* and *purpose* are banished not just from the sphere of inanimate nature, but even from the domain of man and his works. Biological evolution—so it is held—is fundamentally inadequate because all characteristically mental operations involve meaning, value, and purpose—normative factors that evolution banishes from nature's scheme of things. An evolutionary account is accordingly seen as inherently flawed in its elimination of the entire characteristically human dimension of intentionality with its correlatives of meaning, value, and purpose. The evolutionary origin of our thought-mechanisms—it is said—is somehow at odds with an intentional (or purposive or teleological or "spiritual") dimension to our thinking.

Such a position would, of course, cast a shadow of doubt on the adequacy of evolutionary epistemology. For if it were indeed the case that, as a matter of general principle, evolution could not provide for the entire gamut of characteristically mental operations,—or, even worse, stood in conflict therewith—then it would thereby prove itself to be an inherently defective instrumentality of explanation.

(2) The Hermeneutic vs. the Causal Perspective

Such a view is very much mistaken, however. All that is required to operate the process of evolution (along the lines of a Darwinian natural selection) is that there be a heritable, physically transmissible *basis* for the operations of mind by way of the brain as the agency for the neurophysiological processes associated with thinking in its various forms. An evolutionary account of the emergence of mental faculties requires no more than the physical replication over time of creatures whose capacity for mental processes inheres in and results from the operations of their physical endowment. This does indeed mean that our mental functions and performances must be regarded as the *causal product* of our physical equipment and its physical operations. But such a supposition as to their *causal* basis and origins is quite devoid of any implications for their *substantive nature* as ideational processes that involve purpose and meaning. The causal operations of thought processes is one thing, their experienced import quite another.

Evolution brings new qualities to the fore that can transcend their origins. DNA molecules are an assemblage of physical atoms but they encompass the key to organic life—human life included. Birds doubtless initially developed song for signalling warnings of danger, but that did not preclude the evolutionary transmutation of song-behaviors into means for establishing territoriality against potential competition. The physical rooting of an activity or process does not restrict or circumscribe its *functional character.*

The emergence of new modes and levels of operation, function, and behavior that transcend the capabilities of their causal origination is, in fact, characteristic of evolutionary processes. For the first microseconds of cosmic history after the big bang there was no chemistry. The early stages of the universe had no place for biology. There was no foothold in nature for laws of sociology or market-economics before the origin of humans. The emergence of new phenomena at different levels of scale and organizational complexity in nature means the emergence of new processes and laws at these levels. The transition from protophysical to physical and then to chemical and onwards to biological law reflects a succession of new strata of operational complexity. And this holds good for purposive intelligence as well—it is a new phenomenon that emerges at a new level of operational complexity. New products and processes constantly develop from earlier modes of organization, bringing new orders of structure into being. The emergence of the psychological processes that open up realms of meaning and purpose is simply another step in this course of development of new levels of functional complexity.

It is important to bear in mind, however, that while causal explanation proceeds from a mind-external point of view, cognitive functions like meaning, valuing, intending, and the like, can be comprehended *as such* only from within—in the order of hermeneutical understanding. The *physical* processes that lie at the causal basis of thought are, as such, fully open to second-party ("external") examination, description, explanation, modelling. But the *ideational* aspect of thinking can, of course, only be apprehended in one's own first-hand experience (though of course it can be described to others who have similar experiences at their disposal). There is, accordingly, a crucial difference between having a causally productive account of the physical-process concomitants of human mental operations (of the sort that biological evolution provides) and having experiential access to its products "from within." Meaning, intending, and their cousins are all resources that are only at the disposal of someone who also has the appropriate sort of foothold within the realm of mind. Understanding them requires performing them, and performing them requires having a mind that has access to those particular mental experiences. (*Explaining* them, on the other hand, can, in principle, be managed by any sort of sufficiently intelligent being.)

Proper heed of this distinction between the productive causal basis and the descriptive functional nature of mental operations should lead to the recognition that one must not ask an evolutionary account of mind to do the impossible in this regard. Such an account can perfectly well explain the developmental origination of mental operations in terms of their causal basis. But it cannot make their inner experiential character intelligible. The *existence* of mental functions like meaning and purpose can be accounted for on evolutionary principles. But their *qualitative nature* is nevertheless something that can be adequately comprehended only "from within," from a performer's rather than an observer's perspective.

One can fully understand a physical process like the spider's web-weaving without being a spider—without ourselves being in a position to engage in this process and so without knowing what it feels like to perform the activity. But one cannot fully understand a cognitive process like color-vision or symbol-interpretation or anger without *experiencing* that sort of thing. It is one thing to explain how operations originate and another to know what it is like to perform them. The physiology of inebriation can be learned by everyone. But only the person who drinks can comprehend it in the "inner" experiential mode of cognitive access. The mental performances that reflect meaning and purpose can be *understood* only from within the orbit of experience (though their *occurrence* can doubtless be detected and accounted for through external scientific-causal examination). The hermeneutical comprehension of meaning, intending, purposing, valuing, and the like, is bound to experience—to performer's perspective—and thus differs from the neurophysiology of brain processes that is wholly accessible to external observers. The former items reflect issues that evolutionary explanations simply do not address, given their altogether different orientation to the causal dimension of the matter.

(3) Evolutionary Origins

An evolutionary account of the physical processes involved in mental operations is thus by no means reductive (or eliminative) of the inner dimension of intentionality and meaning. In addressing the issue of the physical conditions and processes that engender (that is, *causally* produce) those mental operations at issue with intending, purposing, meaning, etc., it is by its very nature silent regarding their phenomenological character, which can be grasped only "from within." An evolutionary productive/causal account is developed from the angle of the *observer's* perspective, whereas the substantive content of these processes has of necessity to be grasped from within the vantage point of a *performer's* perspective. And of course the former, scientific, evolutionary, neurophysiological account of thought processes does nothing to eliminate or diminish the contentual aspect of meaning and purpose, which can be appreciated only from the "internal," performer's standpoint. But incompleteness is one thing, and defectiveness quite another. The former (evolutionary) account is nowise deficient or defective for failing to provide for the latter (phenomenological/hermeneutic) one—which is *in principle* impossible because of the different levels of consideration that are at issue.

Intentionality (aims and purposes and the like) forms part of the thought-machinery of thinkers, even as mathematical objects such as triangles and spheres do. They do not evolve in nature but come to feature in the operations of (sufficiently sophisticated) minds operating in social interaction. How minds arise and come to acquire their talents and capacities is one thing, what they do with them is another. Biological evolution has to do with the first; intentionality with the second. Evolution operates with respect to the workings of mind—with its processes; intentionality is a matter of its products. There is—and can be—no incompatibility between them, seeing that different issues are involved: biological evolution in the one case, cultural evolution in the other.

All that we can reasonably ask of a biologically evolutionary account of mental operations is that it should explain the emergence of the capacities and processes of thought. The inner phenomenology of thinking lies beyond its range—not because of its deficiencies, but because of the simple fact that it addresses altogether different issues. We cannot fault an evolutionary account of the origination of mind for failing to provide that which no causal account of mind's origination could possibly deliver on its own—cognitive access to the inner, phenomenological nature of mental experience. The nature of the *apparatus* of thought does not restrict the *substance* of our thinking. A Darwinian account of the development of our capacities for mental operation accordingly leaves open scope for purpose and meaning because it does not—and cannot by its very nature—shut the door on issues that it simply does not address. And it clearly cannot be faulted for failing to deal with an issue (viz., the *nature* of understanding and intentionality) that lies entirely outside the range of its causal concerns.

To be sure, then, an evolutionary account of mind is predicated on a position that is "materialistic" in viewing the mind as having a *crucial* basis for its operations in the processes of the body (and the brain in particular).[1] But this sort of causal-origin materialism is nowise at odds with an hermeneutical idealism that maintains that we understand various of the world's processes in terms of concepts and categories drawn from the "inner" experience of the mind's self-observation. Evolution's "mechanical," causal accounting for our *experiences* of purposiveness and intentionality is not in any way at odds with the inner *experienced* aspect of these phenomena. The former issue belongs to the domain of the causal explanation of experiencing as events in the physical world, the latter to the phenomenology of our experiences as phenomena in the world of thought.[2]

The eminent English biologist J.B.S. Haldane once protested, "If my opinions are the result of chemical processes going on in my brain, they are determined by the laws of chemistry, not those of logic."[3] But this argument is surely problematic. If the brain processes involved in opinion formation become (to some extent) aligned, via evolution, to the laws of logic, then clearly it becomes possible to have it both ways. There can be no conflict here. While chemistry (or neurophysiology) may explain how the brain works, "logic" as operative through intentionality and purpose can explain what it does with these capabilities.

A Darwinian account of the origin of mind does not—and by its very nature cannot—conflict with intentionality and purpose because different things are at issue. But of course, it would simply be foolish to deny the originative power of evolutionary processes. To say that a purposive being cannot arise by evolution in a theretofore purpose-lacking world is much like saying that a seeing being cannot arise by evolution in a theretofore vision-lacking world or that an intelligent being cannot arise by evolution in a theretofore intelligence-lacking world. A commitment to the spirit of Darwinism may well impede an acceptance of the purposiveness *of* nature, but it clearly does not and cannot impede an acceptance of purposiveness *in* nature through the evolutionary emergence within nature of beings who themselves have purposes, intentions, goals, etc. No doubt, Darwinian natural selection ill accords with an anthropomorphism of *nature*, but it certainly does not preclude an anthropomorphism of *man*.

The long and short of it is that acceptance of an evolutionary account of the origination and operation of human intelligence leaves ample scope for meaning, value, and purpose in the domain of our human doings and dealings. Did it not do so, its own adequacy would come into question. But it would surely be both naive and mistaken to think that the normative sphere of human assessment is somehow undermined or negated by an account that sees our performance in this domain as rooted in capacities that mankind has acquired through its development in the natural course of evolutionary events. After all, neither our logic nor our mathematics are diminished by noting that the capacity to develop these disciplines is something that has come our way in the evolutionary course of things. Where our intellectual instrumentalities are concerned, the origination of a faculty is surely not at odds with the manner of its operation or the value of its products.

NOTES

1. For a good overview of the philosophical issues involved, see Paul Churchland, *Matter and Consciousness* (Cambridge, Mass.: MIT Press, 1984).

2. Some of these issues are dealt with in greater detail in the author's *Conceptual Idealism* (Oxford: Blackwell, 1973).

3. Quoted in K. R. Popper, *The Open Universe: An Argument for Indeterminism* (Totowa, N.J.: Rowman & Littlefield, 1982), p. 89.

Bibliography

Substantial bibliographies of evolutionary epistemology are appended to the following works:

—Donald T. Campbell, "Evolutionary Epistemology," in P. A. Schilpp (ed.), *The Philosophy of Karl Popper* (La Salle Ill.: Open Court, 1974; "The Library of Living Philosophers" Series), pp. 413–463.

—Franz M. Wuketits, *Concepts and Approaches in Evolutionary Epistemology* (Dordrecht, Boston, Lancaster: Reidel, 1984).

—Gerhard Vollmer, *Evolutionäre Erkenntnistheorie* (3rd ed., Stuttgart, 1984).

—Werner Callebant and Rik Pinxten (eds.), *Evolutionary Epistemology: A Multiparadigmatic Program* (Dordrecht, Boston, Lancaster, Tokyo: Reidel, 1987).

Among the numerous works of the field, I have found the writings of Donald T. Campbell especially lucid and interesting. See in particular his essay on "Natural Selection as an Epistemological Model" in R. Nasoll and R. Cohen (eds.), *A Handbook of Method in Cultural Anthropology* (Garden City: 1970), pp. 51–85. Other books from which I have particularly profited are:

—K. R. Popper, *Objective Knowledge: An Evolutionary Approach* (Oxford: Clarendon Press, 1972).

—Stephen Toulmin, *Human Understanding* (Princeton: Princeton University Press, 1972).

—V. J. Jensen and R. Harré (eds.), *The Philosophy of Evolution* (New York, 1981).

—Robert Boyd and Peter J. Richerson, *Culture and the Evolutionary*

129

Process (Chicago and London: University of Chicago Press, 1985).

—Michael Ruse, *Taking Darwin Seriously* (Oxford: Blackwell, 1986).

—Robert Spaemann, Peter Koslowski, and Reinhard Loew (eds.): *Evolutionstheorie und menschliches Selbstverstaendis: Zur philosophischen Kritik eines Paradigmas moderner Wissenschaft* (Weinheim: Civitas Resultate, Bd. 6 Acta Humaniora, 1984).

—Gerard Radnitzky et al., *Evolutionary Epistemology, Rationality, and the Sociology of Knowledge* (LaSalle, Ill.: Open Court, 1987).

The journal *Biology and Philosophy,* which commenced publication in 1986, regularly carries material of interest.

Additionally to the preceding, the following books have been cited in the text:

Paul Anderson, *Is There Life on Other Worlds?* (New York: Crowell-Collier, 1963).

James Mark Baldwin, *Darwin and the Humanities* (Baltimore: Review Publishing Co., 1909).

Robert Byrd and P. J. Richardson (eds.), *Culture and the Evolutionary Process* (Chicago and London: University of Chicago Press, 1985).

A. G. W. Cameron (ed.), *Interstellar Communication: A Collection of Reprints and Original Contributions* (New York and Amsterdam: W. A. Benjamin, 1963).

Paul Churchland, *Matter and Consciousness* (Cambridge, Mass.: MIT Press, 1984).

P. S. Churchland, *Neurophysiology: Towards a Unified Science for the Mind-Brain* (Cambridge, Mass.: MIT Press, 1986).

J. R. Cole and S. Cole, *Social Stratification in Science* (Chicago: University of Chicago Press, 1973).

Charles Darwin, *The Descent of Man* (New York: A. L. Burt, 1874).

———, *The Origin of Species* (New York: Modern Library, 1952).

Richard Dawkins, *The Blind Watchmaker* (New York: Norton, 1986).

Freeman Dyson, *The Mathematical Sciences* (Cambridge, MA: Cambridge University Press, 1969).

Goesta Ehrensvaerd, *Man on Another World*, tr. by L. and K. Roden (Chicago: University of Chicago Press, 1965).

Albert Einstein, *Lettres à Maurice Solovine* (Paris: Gauthier-Vellars, 1956).

R. B. Goldschmidt, *The Material Basis of Evolution* (New Haven: Yale University Press, 1940).

S. Guttenplan (ed.), *Mind and Language* (Oxford: Clarendon Press, 1975).

J. B. S. Haldane, *Possible Worlds and Other Papers* (New York: Harper & Bros., 1928).

F. A. Hayek, *The Political Order of a Free People* (Chicago: University of Chicago Press, 1979).

Mary Hesse, *Revolutions and Reconstructions in the Philosophy of Science* (Bloomington, Ind.: University of Indiana Press, 1980).

Roland Huntford, *The Last Place on Earth* (New York: Atheneum, 1985).

Christiaan Huygens, *Cosmotheoros: The Celestial Worlds Discovered— New Conjectures Concerning the Planetary Worlds, Their Inhabitants and Productions*, 2nd ed. (London: James Knapton, 1722).

William James, *Pragmatism* (New York: Longmans Green, 1907).

————, *The Will to Believe and Other Essays in Popular Philosophy* (New York: Longmans Green, 1897).

David Kahn, *The Codebreakers* (New York: Macmillan, 1967).

Daniel Kahnemann, Paul Slovic, and Amos Tversky (eds.), *Judgment Under Uncertainty: Heuristics and Biases* (Cambridge: Cambridge University Press, 1982).

G. S. Kirk and J. E. Raven, *The Presocratic Philosophers* (Cambridge: Cambridge University Press, 1957).

Alexandre Koyré, *From the Closed World to the Infinite Universe* (New York: Harper, 1957).

Thomas Kuhn, *The Structure of Scientific Revolutions* (Chicago: University of Chicago Press, 1962).

Thomas Nagel, *Mortal Questions* (Cambridge: Cambridge University Press, 1979).

C. S. Peirce, *Collected Papers*, ed. by C. Hartshorne, P. Weiss, and A. Burks, 8 vols. (Cambridge, Mass.: Harvard University Press, 1931–1958).

Stephen C. Pepper, *The Sources of Value* (Berkeley and Los Angeles: University of California Press, 1958).

Jean Piaget, *The Language and Thought of the Child*, tr. by Marjorie and Ruth Gabain (London: Routledge & Kegan Paul, 1959).

K. R. Popper, *The Open Universe: An Argument for Indeterminism* (Totowa, N.J.: Rowman and Littlefield, 1982).

———, *The Logic of Scientific Discovery* (New York: Basic Books, 1959).

E. Purcell, in *Interstellar Communication: A Collection of Reprints and Original Contributions*, ed. by A. G. W. Cameron (New York: W. A. Benjamin, 1963).

W. V. O. Quine, in Samuel Guttenplan (ed.), *Mind and Language* (Oxford: Clarendon Press, 1975).

———, *Ontological Relativity and Other Essays* (New York: Columbia University Press, 1969).

Nicholas Rescher, *Conceptual Idealism* (Oxford: Blackwell, 1973).

———, *Methodological Pragmatism* (Oxford: Blackwell, 1977).

———, *The Riddle of Existence* (Lanham, Md.: University Press of America, 1984).

———, *Scepticism* (Oxford: Blackwell, 1980).

———, *Scientific Realism* (Dordrecht: Reidel, 1987).

Robert T. Rood and James S. Trefil, *Are We Alone? The Possibility of Extraterrestrial Civilization* (New York: Scribner, 1981).

Louis Rougier, *Traité de la connaisance* (Paris: Gauthier-Villars, 1955).

P. A. Schilpp (ed.), *The Philosophy of Karl Popper* (La Salle, Ill.: Open Court, 1974).

Erwin Schroedinger, *What is Life?* (Cambridge: Cambridge University Press, 1945).

I. S. Shklovskii and Carl Sagan, *Intelligent Life in the Universe,* tr. by Paula Fern (San Francisco: Holden-Day, 1966).

Herbert A. Simon, *The Sciences of the Artificial* (Cambridge, Mass.: MIT Press, 1969).

G. G. Simpson, *This View of Life: The World of an Evolutionist* (New York: Scribner, 1964).

Benjamin Lee Whorf, *Language, Thought, Reality,* ed. by J. B. Carroll (Cambridge, Mass.: Harvard University Press, 1956).

Name Index

136 *Index*

Lorenz, Karl, 11

Mach, Ernst, 13n4
Massey, Gerald, 74n8
Morgan, D. Lloyd, 13n4

Nagel, Thomas, 103n6, 132
Nansen, Fridjtog, 4

Pascal, Blaise, 99
Peirce, Charles Sanders, 5, 11, 30,
    31, 43, 53n4, 60, 93, 103n11,
    132
Pepper, Stephen C., 33n1, 132
Phillips, L. D., 38n17
Piaget, Jean, 132
Popper, K. R., 11–23, 30, 34n2,
    35n5, 57, 74n6, 127n3, 129,
    132
Purcell, E., 103n8, 132

Quine, W. V. O., 74n11, 132

Radnitzky, Gerhardt, 75n11, 130
Raven, J. E., 131
Rescher, Nicholas, 132
Richerson, Peter J., 13n6, 129
Rood, Robert T., 104n17, 132
Rougier, Louis, 53n3, 132
Ruse, Michael, 27, 37n13, 54n6,
    130

Sagan, Carl, 103n13, 133
Schopenhauer, Arthur, 5
Schroedinger, Erwin, 56, 70, 73n2,
    132
Sharpe, Robert, 38n15
Shimony, Abner, 13n5
Shklovskii, I. S., 103n13, 133
Simmel, Georg, 13n4, 84, 103n4
Simon, Herbert A., 37n11, 133
Simpson, George G., 97, 103n15,
    133
Smith, Adam, 51
Solovine, Maurice, 56
Spencer, Herbert, 5, 11

Thagard, Paul, 34n4
Thomson, William (Lord Kelvin),
    35n6
Tigler, Frank J., 102
Toulmin, Stephen, 11, 129
Trefil, James S., 104n17, 132
Tversky, Amos, 38n17

Vaihinger, Hans, 13n4, 37n11
Vollmer, Gerhard, 74n11, 129

Whorf, Benjamin Lee, 103n6, 133
Wigner, Eugene, 56, 73n3
Wuketits, Franz M., 129

Subject Index